Microsoft®
PowerPoint
for Office 365

COPYRIGHT

TRADEMARKS

DISCLAIMER

Product Code: MS POWERPOINT FOR OFFICE 365   19.1

TABLE OF CONTENTS

HOW TO USE THIS MANUAL

This manual was designed to be used as a reference. This is not a step-by-step tutorial. Our feeling is that students did not pay to have someone stand in front of class and <u>read</u> them something that they could do on their own. Through our own classroom experience, we have discovered that students don't read detailed descriptions and that lengthy text is ignored. They prefer to explore and try things out.

In typical tutorials, students often get lost following rote procedures and get caught in error conditions from which they can't back out of. Besides, once students leave class, they just want something they can use to look up a subject quickly without having to read through an entire tutorial. Our design ensures that each course is stimulating and customized yet covers the outlined objectives.

Keys and commands that you need to press are displayed as icons such as ENTER or ↑.

Each topic starts on a new page, making things easy to find and follow. In addition, topics covering actual commands always begin with the USAGE section where we explain the purpose of the command.

PowerPoint has more than one method for accessing its commands. You can use the keyboard using a combination of the function keys and shortcuts, or you can use the mouse by accessing the tools on the Ribbon. You can also use your finger (if you are working on a touch screen device). Not knowing which you would prefer, this book has been written emphasizing mouse and touch commands. Keyboard shortcuts are, however, also included.

The next page shows how a typical topic will be discussed and each part found in the book.

THE TOPIC TITLE WILL BE ON TOP

USAGE:
This part of the manual explains what the command is used for, how it works and other miscellaneous information.

This icon indicates tools or buttons to click on with your mouse.

This part lists the keystrokes and function keys the user may press as a shortcut way of performing the command.

Microsoft PowerPoint supports a whole host of touch-screen gestures, including the swiping, pinching and rotating motions familiar to smartphone and tablet users. Tapping an item opens it; pressing and holding an item pops up a menu to display more information about it (similar to [RIGHT] clicking). This icon indicates a touch-screen gesture.

NOTE:	*This box will tell of things to watch out for. The symbol in the left column always indicates an important note to remember.*

TIP:	*This box will let you in on a little secret or shortcut when working with PowerPoint. When you see this icon, you'll know that a "TIP is available.*

Module One

- **Running PowerPoint**
- **Opening a Presentation**
- **The PowerPoint Screen**
- **Getting Help**
- **Running a Slide Show**
- **The Parts of a Presentation**
- **Changing Views**
- **Working with a Slide**
- **Spell Checking**

RUNNING MICROSOFT POWERPOINT

USAGE:

PowerPoint can be accessed through the Start menu, the Windows desktop or the taskbar (located along the bottom of the desktop).

If you have pinned a shortcut to your desktop, click or tap on the **PowerPoint** icon to run the program.

PowerPoint

If you have pinned it to your taskbar, click on the PowerPoint icon.

If PowerPoint isn't located on the desktop or taskbar, you'll need to display all of your apps (from the Start menu) in order to run it.

Open the Start menu.

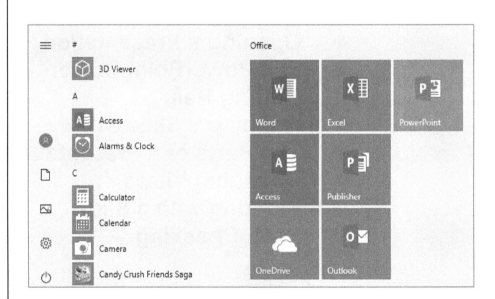

If it isn't already pinned to the Start menu (along the right), scroll through the alphabetical listing of installed apps or click on a letter to display an alphabetical index where you can quickly get to the app based on the first letter of its name.

THE OPENING SCREEN

When you first run the app, you'll be presented with the following screen:

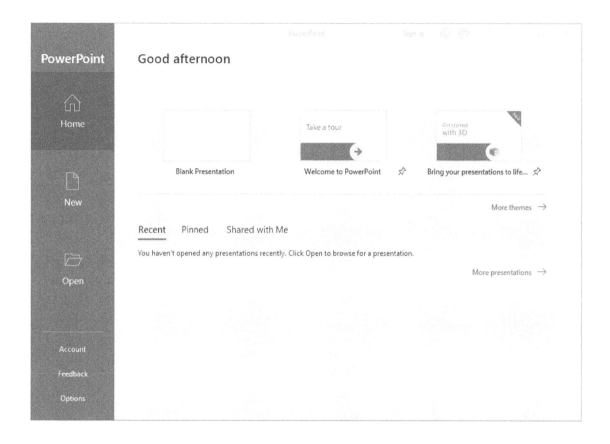

Use **Home** to quickly create a new presentation or open a recent file.

Use **New** to scroll through all of the templates available within PowerPoint. There are several categories of templates (such as Education, Business, Charts, Diagrams, Infographics).

Once you click or tap on one of the themes (from within the **New** section), a pop-up window will open with different color theme options to choose from. There are arrows just outside the borders of the pop-up window. Use these arrows to scroll through other available templates.

Use **Open** to browse your system for an existing presentation.

If you don't see a template that matches the presentation you want to create, you can search for one online.

THE POWERPOINT SCREEN

Once you launch the program and create a new presentation (or open an existing one), you will notice that the program window includes many of the standard elements common to most Office 365 applications as well as a few items that are unique to PowerPoint. The screen can be quite intimidating the first time you see it as there are so many items displayed. However, if you take a few minutes to familiarize yourself with the various screen elements, the program will become easier to work with.

Along the top left corner of the screen is Save tool as well as the Undo, Redo and Slideshow tools. Since those are tools that are most often used, they are placed in a convenient location on what is referred to as the "Quick Access Toolbar".

Click or tap on the button to the right of these tools ▼ to customize this Quick Access Toolbar.

The name of current presentation followed by the application name is displayed in the middle. A generic name is given to each new presentation you create (**Presentation1**).

The right side of the title bar contains the item for signing in to your Microsoft account, along with the Ribbon Display Options button  and three icons for minimizing, maximizing, and closing the program:

This icon (on the next line) allows you to work with others simultaneously on a document. Click on it to quickly share the current document. It also offers live document collaboration to view edits made by other users as they happen.

Allows you to view and respond to comments.

The second line contains tabs which are used to access a series of **Ribbons** to help you quickly find the commands needed to complete a task. Commands are organized in logical groups that are collected together under these tabs. Each tab relates to a type of activity. For example, the View tab contains tools to customize the view. To reduce clutter, some tabs are shown only when needed.

The last item on the ribbon (a magnifying glass with the words "***Tell me what you want to do...***") is an expansive help feature within PowerPoint. This text section allows you to enter words and phrases related to what you want to do next and quickly get to features you want to use or actions you want to perform. You can also choose to get help related to what you're looking for or perform a Smart Lookup - which launches Microsoft's Bing search engine to quickly locate definitions, Wiki articles and other web-related content.

To collapse the ribbon, press CTRL+F1. Press CTRL+F1 a second time to display the ribbon again. Even while collapsed, clicking or tapping on a tab will display the ribbon for that tab

Touch screen users can also display an additional set of commonly used buttons down the right side of the screen (on what is referred to as the **Touch Bar**). To display the Touch Bar, click or tap on ⤓ (on the Quick Access Toolbar) and select Touch/Mouse Mode from the pull-down menu. This will also increase the space between buttons on the ribbon.

The large middle pane contains the currently selected slide and is your actual working area. Directly beneath the working area is yet another pane which can be used to add notes to the current slide.

PowerPoint provides a slide counter along the left side of the **Status Bar** (located at the very bottom of the screen) which lets you know what slide number you are currently viewing/working on.

To the right of the slide counter is an icon  which indicates whether a spelling error has been detected. An *X* will be displayed on this icon when PowerPoint encounters an error.

Towards the right side of the status bar are icons allowing you to hide/display personal notes and/or comments for each slide as well as **View Icons**. The view icons allow you to switch to the various views - depending on what you are doing. For example, normal view is best for adding graphics or editing existing objects while the slide sorter is used to quickly rearrange or delete slides within your presentation. The slide show tool is used to display a visual presentation of all of your slides using various special effects.

Just to the right of the view icons is the **Zoom** area. Notice you can click on the increase **+** or decrease **-** buttons to change the zoom factor. You can also drag the slider horizontally to change the text size as it appears on the screen. PowerPoint displays the current percentage just to the right of this area.

If you zoom to a larger size than can fit vertically or horizontally within the window, vertical and/or horizontal scroll bars will appear along the right side or across the bottom of the screen which can be used to quickly move (vertically) within the current slide.

If you've been playing around with the various zoom factors, click or tap on ⊞ to fit the slide within the current window.

To quickly move to the next or previous slide, PowerPoint provides buttons in the lower right side of the vertical scroll bar. Click or tap on ⯆ to move to the next/previous slide within your presentation.

OPENING A PRESENTATION

USAGE:

Although you will of course be creating presentations from scratch, most of the time you will simply open an existing presentation to view it or to make modifications.

To open an existing presentation, select **Open** from the pull-down list of options within the File tab on the Ribbon.

The following window will be displayed:

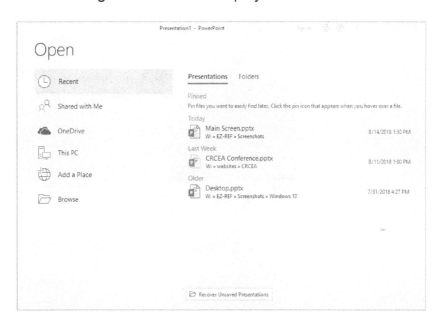

Notice your most recently accessed presentation files are automatically listed in this window.

Your first step is to select where the file is stored:

Recent — This is the default option. PowerPoint automatically displays files you have recently been working on so that you can quickly return to them.

Shared with Me — If you are signed in to your Microsoft account, you can use this option to access documents that have been shared with you.

OneDrive — Use this if you want to open a presentation that has been stored on the Internet rather than a local computer.

This PC — Use this option to open a presentation that was stored in a folder on your local computer – which may also include network locations.

Add a Place — Use this to add a new OneDrive or SharePoint location from which to open files.

> **TIP:** If there are files or folders that you access often, you can "**pin**" them to the list so that they are available whenever you access the Open dialog box.
>
> To pin a file/folder, point to it (from within the list) and then click on the 📌 icon.
>
> If you change your mind and no longer need the file/folder pinned to the list, point to the item and then click on 📌 to remove it.

Browse — If you can't find the folder you need under "This PC", click on the Browse button to search your system for the folder storing the file.

Once you specify where the presentation is located, the following dialog box will be displayed:

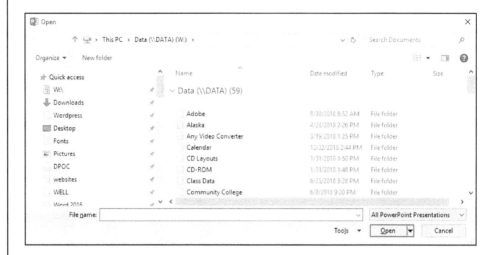

Along the left side of the dialog box, PowerPoint displays the **Navigation Pane**. This pane lists common/favorite locations (links) as well as a section for browsing your folders and drives.

The address bar is displayed, as shown below:

Notice that the path is displayed horizontally on the bar. For example, in the diagram shown above the currently selected location is the "Data" drive (W:) which is on your computer/network. To get to that folder, you had to first choose your computer, then the Data drive (W). You could then select the folder containing your PowerPoint files.

This layout is commonly referred to as "bread crumbs" because it shows you the path that was taken to get to the current location.

In the example shown on the previous page, you can easily move to another folder on the "W" drive by clicking or tapping on ⟩ beside the drive name and then selecting a different folder to view.

Across the top of the window are the following buttons:

Organize ▼   Click or tap this button to access the **Organize** pull-down menu. From the pull-down list, select the operation (e.g., cut, copy, paste, delete, rename) you want to perform on existing files listed within this box.

New folder   Click or tap this button to create a new folder.

When ready, double-click or double-tap on the name of the file you want to open or highlight the name and click/tap   Open ▼ .

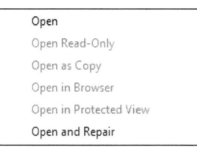

If you click or tap the down arrow ▼ beside the Open ▼ button, you can choose from a list of options (such as opening the file as read-only or in your Web browser).

TIP:	To open more than one presentation at a time, select the first file by clicking on its name once to highlight it. Next, hold the *CTRL* key down as you click on each additional file to be opened. Once all files have been selected, click or tap Open ▼ to actually open them. Each file will be placed in its own window.

TIP:	The shortcut key for opening files from within the presentation itself is *CTRL*+*O*.

SWITCHING BETWEEN MULTIPLE FILES

When working with two or more open presentations, you can access the **View** ribbon and click on the button labeled **Switch Windows** and then select the file you want to switch to.

Alternatively, you can quickly switch between open presentations using the Windows taskbar (located along the bottom of your screen):

Either point or click on the icon to display a preview of each of your opened presentations, as shown below:

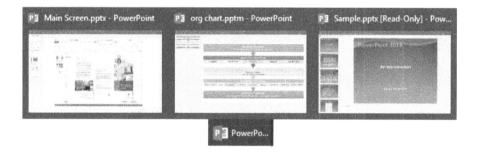

Simply click on the presentation you wish to work with.

WORKING WITH HELP

USAGE:

PowerPoint has expanded and improved its Help feature in Office 365, now offering quick and extensive help without you having to do more than enter the item you need help on.

Using the **Tell me** search bar, simply enter the function or feature you're looking for and PowerPoint will offer the function itself (rather than a help page describing it).

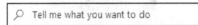

Click or tap in this section (located to the right of the ribbons) and type your question.

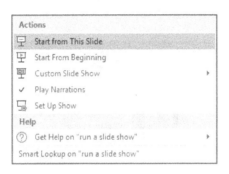

As you begin typing, PowerPoint will display help on that topic. If PowerPoint finds the related commands for that topic, it displays them in the pull-down menu.

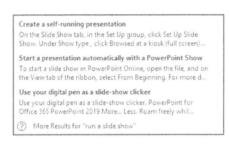

If none of the commands listed are what you want, click on the "Get Help" section to find more detailed information on that item.

Use "Smart Lookup" to open the Insights pane (powered by Bing) to locate definitions, Wiki articles, and top related searches from the web.

Clicking on one of the items within the "Get Help on …" submenu displays a new panel along the right side of your screen:

This panel displays help on the item you selected.

Scroll through the step-by-step instructions and diagrams.

The article may include links to related help topics.

Some links may require Internet access as they will attempt to launch your Internet browser and access Microsoft's support website.

←   Click on this arrow to return to the previous help screen.

…   Click on the three dots (…) to display a pull-down menu with the following items:

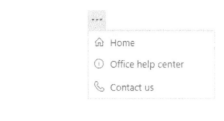

   Click or tap in this box to enter a new search topic

At the end of each help topic, you will see two items:

One item will allow you to send feedback to Microsoft as to whether the information contained within the help panel was helpful:

After answering the question, you can also include a comment as part of the feedback you are sending Microsoft:

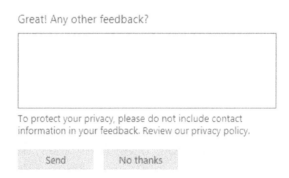

The second item (at the bottom of the help panel) allows you to launch your Internet browser and view more detailed information on the currently selected topic through Microsoft's support website:

Read article in browser ⌐'

You can then use your browser's print option if you'd like to print out information on the selected topic.

EXITING HELP

 Click or tap this button (located in the top right corner) to **close** the help window and return to your presentation.

SCREENTIPS

A common problem most users encounter is not knowing what each tool on the screen represents.

For example, the SAVE tool is displayed as a 3.5" diskette which some users do not immediately relate to saving a file.

To alleviate this problem, PowerPoint offers quick mouse assistance on each tool, referred to as ScreenTips.

 As you point to a tool, PowerPoint will display a quick note as to the tool's function.

RUNNING A SLIDE SHOW

USAGE:

A slide show is a desktop presentation. They are most often used when presenting information to an audience. Slide shows can be instrumental in conveying your message to a group of people since graphics can help make it more understandable.

You can connect your PC to an overhead projector and display the show to a large group of people or it can be used on the PC in front of a small group (i.e., a sales presentation). It can either be running in the background as you speak to the group or you can add enough special effects and sound that the show itself is sufficient in conveying the point you are trying to make.

Rather than simply showing the audience a set of boring slides, including animation and special effects give the presentation added appeal so that the slides hold the audience's attention while still making a dramatic point.

It is possible to control the flow of the show using either the keyboard or the mouse. It can be a self-running demonstration or can run interactively with the audience depending on your requirements. You can also change the sequence of the slides in the middle of the show if needed.

Running a slide show displays each of the slides contained within a presentation file one at a time on the computer screen. You can determine an **automatic** time interval between slides being drawn on the screen or you can instruct PowerPoint that you want to **manually** determine the speed each of the slides is drawn.

If you run it manually, you can use the mouse or keyboard to move between slides.

Another nice feature is the ability to **Rehearse** the times between slides by previewing the show and setting individual times for each slide of the presentation.

STARTING A SLIDE SHOW

 Click or tap this tool (located with the view buttons – towards the right side of the status bar) to start the slide show from the current slide.

 Click or tap this tool (located on the Quick Access bar at the top of your screen) to start the slide show from the beginning.

PowerPoint will immediately begin displaying the slide show - with the first slide taking up the full screen.

MOVING AROUND WITHIN THE SLIDE SHOW

 Click or tap this tool (located with the other slide show tools in the bottom left corner of the slide show screen) or click the **[LEFT]** mouse button to display the next slide.

 Click or tap this button (located with the other slide show tools in the bottom left corner of the slide show screen) to display the previous slide.

NOTE:	*If you don't see the navigation bar, move your mouse and then look in the bottom left corner of the slide show. The tools are very light in color so that they do not distract from the slide show.*

Press ⊥ or PG↓ to move to the next slide.

Press ↑ or PG↑ to move to the previous slide.

Press HOME to move to the first slide or END to go to the last.

Press ESC to cancel the show.

USING THE PEN

By default, when you click the **[LEFT]** mouse button while viewing a slide show, the next slide within the presentation will be displayed. However, if you prefer, you can assign a pen or highlighter to the **[LEFT]** mouse button to emphasize points as the show is running.

To do so, click your **[RIGHT]** mouse button (from within the slide show) and choose "Pointer Options" from the pop-up menu.

You can also click or tap on the ⊘ tool (which is located with the other slide show tools along the bottom left of your slide show screen).

A pop-up menu will be displayed, as shown below:

Select the type of pen or highlighter you would like to use to annotate your slides during the show.

Notice you can also choose a different **Ink Color**. The default color is black but you can choose any other color from the list provided.

After selecting a pen or highlighter, the function of the **[LEFT]** mouse button will have changed so that you may now begin annotating the slides during the show.

Once the pen or highlighter has been enabled, you will need to use the arrow tools (located with the other slide show tools along the bottom left side of the slide show screen) to move to the next or previous slide.

If you realize you have added too many annotations with the pen or highlighter, you can erase them by clicking or tapping the ✐ tool.

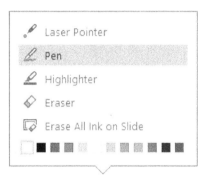

From the pop-up menu, choose **Erase All Ink on Slide** to erase all annotations you have added to the slide or select **Eraser** to manually erase only some of the annotations from the slide. If you choose the Eraser option, the pointer will change to an eraser so that you can click and drag to erase the unwanted marks.

To disable the pen or eraser, click or tap on ✐ and deselect the tool from the pop-up menu.

CHANGING VIEWS

USAGE:

The PowerPoint screen is divided into three basic panes. The leftmost pane is most often used to display thumbnails of each slide within your presentation while the large middle pane displays the currently selected slide. The pane beneath the working area is used for adding and displaying slide notes.

To switch between the various views, PowerPoint offers a series of buttons located along the bottom right of the screen. Each view has its advantages.

 The **Notes** option allows you to quickly add notes to the current slide that can be printed.

 The **normal** view is best used to show the outline and current slide simultaneously.

 The **slide sorter** view is best used to view the entire presentation at once, rearrange the slides, copy and move slides between presentations and delete slides from the presentation.

 The **reading** view is used to display the slide show within the current window size rather than a full screen.

 The **slide show** view is best used to preview your presentation to verify the timing and transition methods between slides.

CHANGING THE VIEWING SIZE

Along the status bar (just to the right of the viewing icons) is the **Zoom** area. Notice you can click or tap on the increase **+** or decrease **-** buttons to change the zoom factor.

 131%

You can also drag the slider horizontally to change the slide size as it appears on the screen. PowerPoint displays the current percentage just to the left of this area.

WORKING WITH THE SLIDE SORTER

The **Slide Sorter** displays a thumbnail sketch of each of your slides so that you can easily see them all at once. These miniature slides are spread across several rows on a single screen (whenever possible).

This view is the quickest way to move slides around and delete unwanted slides.

Click or tap this button (located with the other view buttons along the bottom right side of the screen) to access the **Slide Sorter** view.

The outline/slide pane closes to expand the working area so that you can display several slides at once, as shown below:

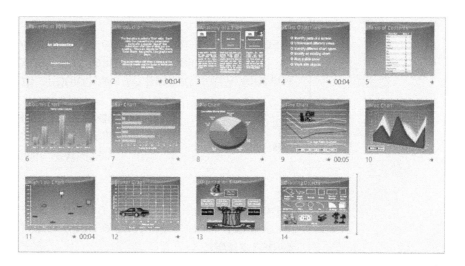

If you have assigned a transition to a slide (such as assigning a fade effect when it loads during the slide show), you will see a star at the bottom of the slide. If you have set a timing for a slide, it will also be displayed underneath the slide.

REARRANGING SLIDES

You can rearrange the slides within the slide sorter by simply dragging them to a new location. As you begin dragging a slide, a thin vertical line is displayed to indicate where the slide will be placed when you release the mouse button.

DELETING AN UNWANTED SLIDE

To delete an unwanted slide, simply click or tap on it once (from the outline pane along the left side of the window to select it) and then press the DEL key.

GRAYSCALE VS COLOR

If your presentation is made up of many slides and you know you'll be printing in black and white, you can check out how your slides will look when printed by switching to grayscale or black and white.

Click or tap one of these buttons (located within the **Color/Grayscale** section on the View Ribbon) to switch to grayscale or pure black and white.

Once you select grayscale or black and white, the ribbon changes to display various grayscale options to further customize individual slide objects.

Once you have chosen grayscale or black and white, click/tap this button to return to color view.

WORKING WITH NOTES

The **Notes** view displays the actual slide in the top half of the screen and then leaves an area at the bottom for speaker notes. These notes can be printed as a reference for the speaker to help them with the presentation as they deliver it or can be left blank and handed out to the audience so that they can write their own comments as the presentation is being delivered.

≜ Notes   To show/hide the **Notes** section, click or tap this button (located along the status bar at the bottom of your screen).

The screen changes to display the slide with an area at the bottom for notes, as shown in the diagram below:

Before entering your notes, you might want to switch to a larger viewing size by clicking or tapping on the increase **+** button (located just to the right of the current zoom factor **100%** along the bottom right side of the screen).

WORKING WITH COMMENTS

When you select **Comments**, a new window pane is opened along the right side of your screen which can be useful when collaborating with other users.

Simply open the Comments pane and add whatever comments you wish to the slide(s).

💬 Comments   To open the **Comments** pane, click or tap this button (located towards the upper right corner of your screen – just above the Ribbon bar).

The screen changes to display the slide with an area along the right side of the screen for comments, as shown in the diagram below:

WORKING WITHIN THE SLIDE PANE

Since the slide pane is set as the largest pane within PowerPoint, it is important that you understand the screen elements present when working within this pane.

Notice along the bottom left side of the screen (on the status bar) that PowerPoint indicates the current slide number.

Along the bottom right side of the slide (on the vertical scroll bar) are two buttons which can be used to quickly move to the previous and next slide within the presentation.

 Click or tap either of these two buttons to move to the **previous** or **next** slide.

Along the right side of the slide, PowerPoint displays a vertical scroll bar which can be used to move to specific slides.

Drag the rectangular scroll box up or down to display the desired slide number/name.

Notice as you drag, that a small text box shows the number and title of the slide that would be displayed if you were to release the mouse button.

SPELL CHECKING A PRESENTATION

USAGE:

Before finalizing a presentation, you should take advantage of PowerPoint's spell-checking feature.

Not only does it check for misspellings, but it will also alert you of repeated words and incorrect capitalization.

The program comes with a main dictionary, but you can add words to your own personal dictionary.

abc
✓
Spelling

Click or tap the **Spelling** tool (located within the **Proofing** section on the Review Ribbon) or click on the 📖 icon (located on the status bar at the bottom of your screen).

The following panel is opened along the right side of the screen:

PowerPoint will stop at the first unrecognized word, highlight it, and offer suggestions.

The following buttons are provided within the spell-checking panel:

 If the word should remain as it is, select the **Ignore** button. PowerPoint also offers the option of **Ignore All** if the word in question appears throughout the presentation.

 If the word should be added to your custom dictionary for future reference, click on this button.

 If one of the suggestions is correct, double-click or double-tap on the correct spelling or highlight the word and choose the **Change** button. If you are afraid you misspelled a word more than once, click or tap the **Change All** button.

 Along the bottom half of the panel, PowerPoint provides an option to pronounce the selected word by clicking or tapping on this icon.

Notice that PowerPoint also provides a list of synonyms (if available) for the currently selected word.

 ✕ Click or tap this button to remove the panel from the screen.

After running the spell checker, you will want to save your presentation with all of the corrections.

Module Two

- **Selecting Objects**
- **Moving/Copying Objects**
- **Deleting Selected Objects**
- **Working with Fonts**
- **Changing Colors**

SELECTING OBJECTS

USAGE:

Once objects have been added to a slide, you must select them before modification is possible. PowerPoint allows you to move, copy, resize, delete and change the color of the selected object. If the object contains text, you may also edit the font and size of the text, as well as any attributes that may have been applied.

 Move to the edge of unfilled objects or to the middle of filled pictures. Once you see the pointer change to a four-way arrow, click the **[LEFT]** mouse button.

An object is selected when it has the outline of a box with small circular handles. A rotation handle appears at the top of the selected object.

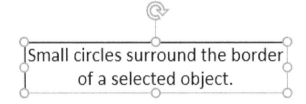

Small circles surround the border of a selected object.

SELECTING MULTIPLE OBJECTS

To select multiple objects, click on the first object and then hold the SHIFT key down while clicking on additional objects.

NOTE:	If you click on an object a second time (while holding SHIFT down), you will be deselecting that object.

TIP:	You can also click or tap in an empty area and drag a rectangle around all the objects to select. PowerPoint selects all objects enclosed within the rectangle.

SELECTING ALL OBJECTS

To select all of the objects currently on the slide:

 Select ▾   Click or tap this tool (located within the **Editing** section of the Home Ribbon).

   From the pull-down list, choose **Select All**.

If you prefer using the keyboard:

 CTRL + A

All objects within the slide should now be selected.

To **unselect** specific objects, hold the SHIFT key down and click the objects that you do not want to include in the group.

THE SELECTION PANE

To select, rename or hide objects on the slide:

 Select ▾   Click or tap this button (located within the **Editing** section of the Home Ribbon).

   From the pull-down list, choose **Selection Pane...**

The right side of the screen will display a list of all the objects on the slide. You can select individual or multiple objects, or you can hide/show objects by clicking or tapping on the eye ☁ .

You can also rename an object by clicking or tapping on its current name and then clicking/tapping a second time to edit the existing name.

The reorder arrows are used to change the priority of overlapping objects.

MOVING OBJECTS

USAGE:

You can move objects around on the slide by dragging them from one location to another using your mouse, as outlined in the steps shown below.

❶ 　Move to the middle (of an online picture or filled object) or the edge (for unfilled objects) of the selected item.

　　　　If using a mouse, be sure that the mouse pointer changes to the four-way arrow.

　　　　Click or tap and then drag the object to its new location.

❷　　Once you reach the new location, release the mouse button (or your finger if working with a touch screen device) and the original object will appear in its new location.

| TIP: | You can also move an object by selecting it and then clicking or tapping on ✂ Cut (located within the **Clipboard** section of the Home Ribbon). To paste it in a new location, click or tap the 📋 Paste tool.

This method is used when moving an object from one slide or presentation to another. |

PRACTICE EXERCISE

Instructions:	❶	Move to slide number 9 in the presentation.
	❷	Move the clipart picture to the bottom right of the graph.
	❸	Move the graph title to the top center of the graph.

The slide should look similar to the one shown below.

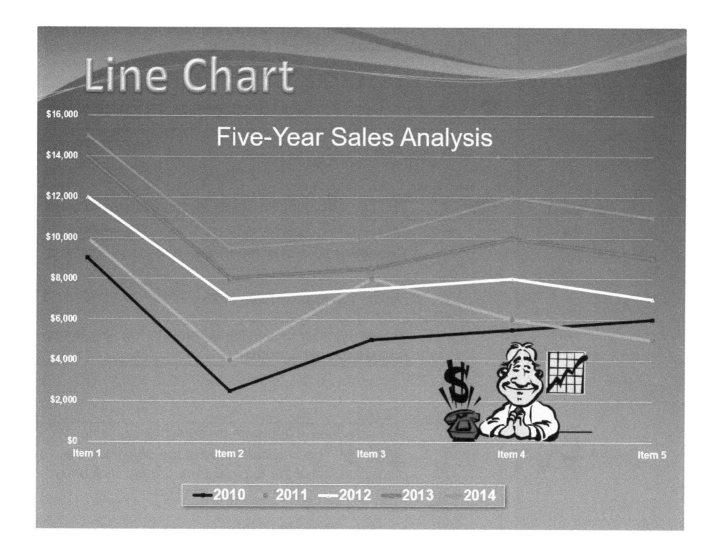

COPYING OBJECTS

USAGE:

To copy an object within your presentation, follow these steps:

❶ Move to the middle (of an online picture or filled object) or the edge (for unfilled objects) of the selected item. Be sure that the mouse pointer changes to the four-way arrow.

Hold down the **CTRL** key. You'll see a small plus symbol (**+**) on the mouse pointer. Continue to hold the **CTRL** key down while dragging the object to its new location. As you drag the object, notice that a transparent copy of the object is dragged with the mouse pointer.

❷ Once you reach your destination, release the mouse button and then the **CTRL** key. The original object will be copied to its new location.

> *TIP:*   *You can also copy an object by selecting it and then clicking or tapping on* ⧉ Copy *(located within the* **Clipboard** *section of the Home Ribbon). To paste it, click or tap the* Paste *tool.*
>
> *This is used when copying an object from one slide or presentation to another.*

> *TIP:*   *You can quickly duplicate an object by pressing* **CTRL**+**D***. The duplicate copy of the object will be placed on top of the original item. Simply click and drag the duplicate to its new location.*
>
> *Once you move the duplicate, you can press* **CTRL**+**D** *again (as many times as you like). PowerPoint will automatically use the spacing between the original object and the first duplicate to evenly distribute additional duplicates.*

USING THE OFFICE CLIPBOARD

USAGE:

You can use the Office Clipboard to collect multiple items (both text and graphics) to be pasted within PowerPoint or other Office applications.

The standard Windows clipboard is only able to store one item at a time. You have to paste whatever you have cut or copied before your next cut/copy can be completed.

However, the Office Clipboard can store up to 24 items at a time, making it easy to collect multiple items to be pasted. If you copy a 25th item, the first item in your clipboard will automatically be removed to make room for the latest entry.

Depending on your computer's settings, choosing to copy an item and then copying a second one without pasting the first may trigger the Clipboard task pane to be displayed.

If the task pane is not automatically displayed, you can manually display it by accessing the following tool:

Click or tap the **Clipboard Task Pane Launcher** (located along the far left side of the Home Ribbon).

The Office Clipboard will automatically be opened and placed within a task pane, as shown below:

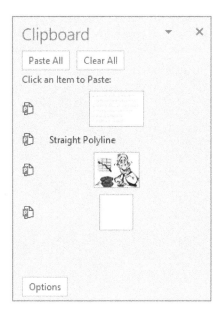

The clipboard will display each of the cut or copied items - with the latest item placed at the top of the list.

If you have cut or copied several entries, a scroll bar will be placed along the right side so that you can quickly move through the items.

A small icon is placed to the left of each object to indicate what application the cut or copied item was originally created in.

Move to the location to which the item(s) should be pasted.

Click or tap the clipboard item to be pasted.

There are two tools available across the top of the clipboard:

     Click or tap this tool to paste each of the items stored within the Office Clipboard in the current presentation (or within the current Office application).

     Click or tap this button to clear the contents of the Office Clipboard. It will also clear the Windows Clipboard.

To remove a single item from the clipboard, point to the item you want to remove until you see a small down arrow ⊡.

   Click or tap the down arrow ⊡ and select **Delete** from the list of options.

CLIPBOARD OPTIONS

Towards the bottom of the clipboard is a button <u>Options</u> which is used to change the display settings for the Office Clipboard.

Show Office Clipboard Automatically
Show Office Clipboard When Ctrl+C Pressed Twice
Collect Without Showing Office Clipboard
✓ Show Office Clipboard Icon on Taskbar
✓ Show Status Near Taskbar When Copying

From the five options available, check the box labeled **Show Office Clipboard Automatically** to open the clipboard within the task pane when two items in a row have been copied.

Select **Show Office Clipboard When Ctrl+C Pressed Twice** to display the Office Clipboard after pressing the copy shortcut keys.

Choose **Collect Without Showing Office Clipboard** if you prefer not to display the clipboard within the task pane when two items in a row have been copied. This option displays the clipboard icon on the taskbar even if you are in a different application. Make sure the first two options have not been checked.

Select **Show Office Clipboard Icon on Taskbar** to display the clipboard icon at the bottom of your screen.

Choose **Show Status Near Taskbar When Copying** to display the status of a copied item on the taskbar.

Check each of the options you would like to enable from the list. Click a second time to disable the option.

Once the Office Clipboard has been activated, an icon will be placed on the Windows taskbar (notification tray) along the bottom right of your screen.

If you don't see the Office Clipboard icon on your taskbar, it may be one of the hidden items. Click on ^ to view the hidden items.

If you right-click or tap and hold (if using a touch screen) on the clipboard icon located along the taskbar at the bottom of your screen, the following list of options will be displayed:

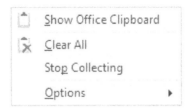

From this list, you can choose to display the Office Clipboard, clear all of the items currently being stored within the clipboard, or close the clipboard. The last item within this list allows you to specify the display options for the clipboard (which were discussed on the previous page).

If you do not specify otherwise, the collected items remain in the Clipboard until you close all Office applications.

RESIZING OBJECTS

USAGE:

PowerPoint allows you to easily change an object's size - keeping its original proportions or changing its shape as you resize.

To resize an object, follow the steps outlined below:

❶ Select the object to resize.

❷ ⟷ ↕ ⤡ ⤢ Move the mouse so the tip of the arrow touches one of the surrounding round handles (white circles). The pointer will change to one of these double-sided arrows

❸ Use one of the four corner handles to change the object's height and width at the same time.

❹ When done, release the button.

NOTE:	*Dragging the handles of a text item only serves to change the left or right margins of the text block. This may cause the text to wrap within the margins.*

PRACTICE EXERCISE

Instructions:

❶ Open the **Sample** presentation and move to slide number 3. Copy the California flag.

❷ Move to slide number 9 and paste the flag on that slide. Move the flag to the upper right corner of the slide.

❸ Replace the happy salesman with the worried salesman picture from slide 14.

❹ Make the entire graph a little shorter to make more room at the top of the slide.

❺ Move the title outside of the graph.

The slide should look similar to the one shown below.

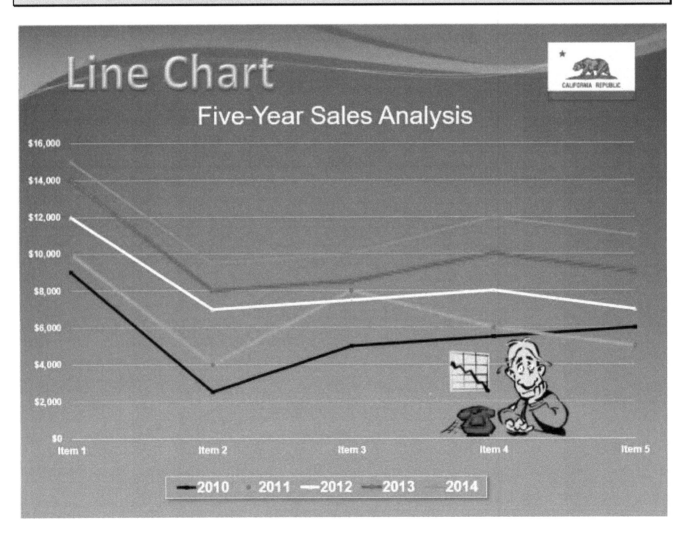

ARRANGING OBJECTS

USAGE:

PowerPoint allows you to arrange objects on your slide in a number of ways. For example, you might have two items that overlap one another and decide that one of the objects needs to be placed behind the other. In that case, you would choose to send the object back or choose to bring the other object forward. Once the two objects have been arranged properly, you can then group them into one object so that you can easily move them without worrying about the multiple layers.

Since graphic objects can be placed anywhere on a slide, they can at times be placed on top of each other - thereby overlapping. This can be used to combine several layers of objects to create special effects or even a new picture. For example, the picture below started out with a picture of a dog carrying a newspaper. The text was then added and placed on top of the newspaper.

To do this, you would simply add the text within a text box and then drag the text box on top of the dog picture.

However, you may find that when you drag one object on top of another they are overlapped incorrectly, as shown below:

BRINGING AN OBJECT FORWARD

❶ Select the object to be placed on top of the other(s).

❷  Click or tap the down arrow ⊡ beside this button (located within the **Arrange** section of the Format Ribbon). If you have more than two objects overlapping, you may want the item brought to the very front.

SENDING AN OBJECT BACK

❶ Select the object to be placed behind the other(s).

❷  Click or tap the down arrow ⊡ beside this button (located within the **Arrange** section of the Format Ribbon) to choose whether the selected object should be sent back one layer at a time. If you have more than two objects overlapping, you may want the selected item sent behind all others.

GROUPING MULTIPLE OBJECTS

After arranging the objects so they look like one picture, you may decide that you should group them as one object so that if you decide to move the item, all objects move together.

❶ Select each of the objects you want to group as one item.

❷  Click or tap the down arrow ⊡ beside this button (located within the **Arrange** section of the Format Ribbon) to group each of the selected objects. Notice if you group multiple objects by mistake you can choose to ungroup them using this same pull-down menu.

ALIGNING MULTIPLE OBJECTS

PowerPoint also allows you to align multiple items on a slide. For example, you may want the tops of each selected object to line up or the center point of each object to be aligned. You can also choose to align them evenly on the slide.

❶   Select each of the objects you want to align.

❷   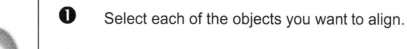 Click or tap the down arrow ⊡ beside this button (located within the **Arrange** section of the Format Ribbon) to specify the alignment.

ROTATING OBJECTS

You can also choose to rotate or flip an object on the slide. For example, to create a more custom look you might decide that an item looks better at an angle or even flipped to another side.

❶   Select the object to be rotated.

❷   ⟲ Rotate ⁓   Click or tap the down arrow ⊡ beside this button (located within the **Arrange** section of the Format Ribbon) to rotate or flip an object.

TIP:	*You can also rotate an object by grabbing this handle*
	(located at the top of the object when it is selected) and dragging left or right to rotate the object.

DELETING OBJECTS

USAGE:

There may be times while editing a slide that you decide that an object is no longer needed and should be removed entirely.

❶   Select the object(s) to be deleted.

❷   Press the ⌊DEL⌋ key and the object(s) will be removed.

OOPS! UNDELETING

If you mistakenly delete an object from a slide, PowerPoint allows you to undo the deletion, as shown below:

↻▾   Click or tap on this tool (located on Quick Access toolbar) to **Undo** the last action. To undo more than one action, click or tap the down arrow ▾ beside the tool.

> *TIP:*   *PowerPoint's Undo feature includes the last 20 actions but can be increased to a maximum of 150. To modify the default value, click on the File tab on the Ribbon and select Options from the pull-down list. From the resulting window, choose **Advanced**. Editing options are the first set of options within the Advanced Options section.*

REDOING AN ACTION

If you delete an item and then undo the deletion and then realize you really did want to delete that item, PowerPoint allows you to redo the last action.

↻   Click or tap on this tool (located on the Quick Access toolbar) to **Redo** the last action.

CUSTOMIZING OBJECTS

USAGE:

Once an item has been placed onto the slide, you may want to customize its appearance. You can change the color of the lines surrounding an object, the fill color or pattern within the object, add shading or even apply 3D effects to some objects.

The quickest way to customize a shape is to use one of the predefined settings.

Once the object has been selected, display the Format Ribbon and then select one of the options provided within the Styles section, as shown below. The styles and colors available will vary depending according to the type of object you have selected (i.e., line vs text) as well as the presentation's theme.

Click or tap the ⬚ button to display the full list of styles:

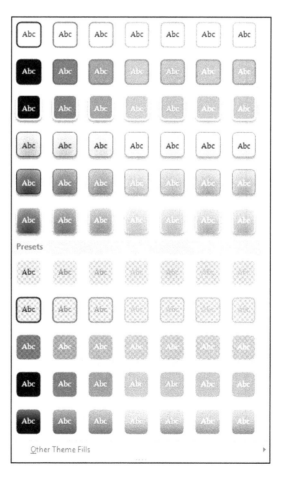

CHANGING OUTLINE/LINE COLOR AND STYLE

To modify the color applied to the outline as well as the style of the line, follow the steps below:

❶   Select the object(s) to be modified.

❷   ✎ Shape Outline ▾   Click or tap this tool (located within the **Drawing** section on the Home Ribbon).

❸

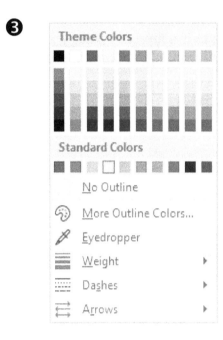

From this pull-down list, you can choose a new outline color, remove the outline altogether, change the weight of the outline, and change the style of the line to include dashes or arrows.

If you do not see the desired color from the list, select **More Outline Colors...** which displays the entire color palette.

Notice as you move your mouse over each of the options within the list, PowerPoint provides a preview of the selected object using the option you are currently pointing to.

CHANGING FILL COLORS

To modify the fill color, picture, gradient, and texture applied to an object, follow the steps outlined below:

❶   Select the object(s) to be modified.

❷      Click or tap this tool (located within the **Drawing** section on the Home Ribbon).

❸   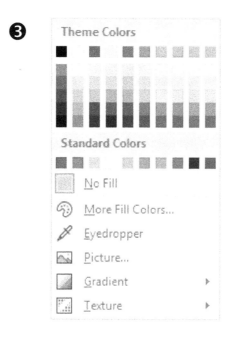   From this pull-down list, you can choose a new fill color, remove the fill altogether, or change the fill to include a picture, a gradient, or a texture.

If you do not see the desired color from the list, select **More Fill Colors...** which displays the entire color palette.

Notice as you move your mouse over each of the options within the list, PowerPoint provides a preview of the selected object using the option you are currently pointing to.

A gradient typically consists of two colors gradually blending from one color to the other. You can select the colors to be used as well as the intensity and the direction in which the gradient will be generated.

Textures are basically small patches of patterns that resemble real-life textures such as marble, cloth, grass, paper, wood, etc.

Rather than using one of the built-in textures or patterns, you can also choose to fill an object with a custom picture. PowerPoint recognizes most graphic file formats to provide you with a wide variety of options.

ADDING A SHAPE EFFECT

Adding a shape effect (such as a shadow or a bevel effect) can give an object a more custom look and feel to help it to stand out from the rest of the drawing.

To apply a shape effect to an object, follow the steps below:

❶   Select the object(s) to be modified.

❷   🗂 Shape Effects ▾   Click or tap on this tool (located within the **Drawing** section on the Home Ribbon).

❸

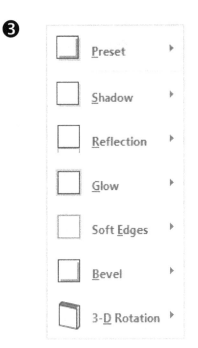

From this pull-down list, choose the shape effect you wish to apply to the selected object.

Notice as you move your mouse over each of the options within the list, PowerPoint provides a preview of the selected object using the option you are currently pointing to.

PRACTICE EXERCISE

Instructions:	❶	Move to slide number 13.
	❷	Select the box containing the president's name and change the **Fill** color to a dark blue and change the **Line** color to a light blue.
	❸	Select the boxes containing the vice presidents and change the **Fill** color to a light green and add a white dashed border.
	❹	Select the two managers at the bottom of the chart and change the **Fill** color to a maroon color and apply a bevel effect to those boxes.
	❺	Change the color of the connecting lines to yellow.

WORKING WITH TEXT

USAGE:

You can also change the attributes of text, such as the font, size, color and style. First, select the text to be edited by clicking the pointer on the text item that you want to edit. You can also select a single word or group of characters from within a text object.

 To select an entire text object, click or tap it once. The first time you click, you will be able to edit the text or highlight just a portion of the text to be modified.

If you click or tap a second time (this time on the border surrounding the text), you will select the entire text object. Do not click the second time until you see the pointer change shape to a four-way arrow.

CHANGING FONTS

After having selected the text object to be changed:

❶ | Calibri ▾ | Click or tap the down arrow ▾ (located to the right of the font tool within the **Font** section of the Home Ribbon). Notice that PowerPoint displays a preview of each font in the list so you can see how the font looks before selecting it. If you hover your mouse over the font name, PowerPoint will also provide a preview of that font on the selected object on your slide.

❷ Select the desired font from the pull-down list.

CHANGING POINT SIZE

❶ Click or tap the down arrow ▾ beside the font size tool.

❷ | 11 ▾ | Select the desired size from the pull-down list.

CHANGING THE FONT THROUGHOUT A PRESENTATION

Not only can you change the font for a single text object on a slide but PowerPoint also allows you to quickly replace the font throughout the entire presentation. For example, if you created a number of slides using Times New Roman and now decide you should have used Arial, you can quickly replace each instance of the Times New Roman font with Arial throughout the entire presentation.

Click or tap this tool (located within the **Editing** section on the Home Ribbon).

From the pull-down list, choose **Replace Fonts...**

The following dialog box will be displayed:

In the box labeled **Replace**, click or tap the down arrow ∨ and select the current font that you want to replace.

In the box labeled **With**, click on the down arrow ∨ and select the font you want to substitute the current font for.

Click or tap Replace to actually replace the font.

The dialog box will remain open so you can continue to replace fonts. When done, click or tap Close to close the dialog box.

APPLYING ATTRIBUTES

To emphasize text within a slide you may use the bold, underline, or italics attributes. You can also apply strikethrough, for example, to show a previous number that has been changed.

Begin by selecting the text object(s) to be modified.

Once the text has been selected, you can either use the mouse (selecting the buttons contained within the **Font** section of the Home Ribbon) or the keyboard to apply the attributes.

B   Click or tap this tool to turn **bold** on and off.

I   Use this tool to turn *italics* on and off.

U̲   Click or tap this tool to turn underline on and off.

S   Click or tap this tool to add/remove a shadow effect.

a̶b̶   Use this tool to turn ~~strikeout~~ on and off.

A⃗V⃖   Click or tap this tool to change the character spacing.

Aa ▾   Use this tool to specify upper/lower case.

A̲ ▾   Click or tap this tool to change the font color.

A^ A˅   Click or tap these tools to **increase**/decrease the font size.

If you prefer using the keyboard, select the text object to be modified and then press one of the following shortcut keys:

CTRL + B   This key combination is used to apply **bold**.

CTRL + I   This key combination is used to apply *italics*.

CTRL + U   This key combination is used to apply underline.

SHADOWING TEXT

To further enhance your text, you can add a shadow effect by following the steps outlined below:

❶   Select the text object to modify.

❷   S   Click or tap this button (located within the **Font** section of the Home Ribbon) to add/remove shadowing.

CHANGING FONT COLOR

To change the color of a text object, follow these steps:

❶   Select the text item to be modified.

❷   A ▾   Click or tap this tool to use the last selected color or click or tap on the down arrow ⊡ beside the **Font Color** tool (located within the Font section on the Home Ribbon) to choose another font color.

❸   Select the color you want to use (from the pull-down list) for the selected text.

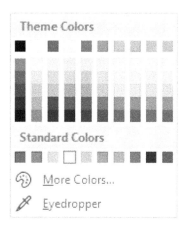

To view the complete color palette, click or tap on 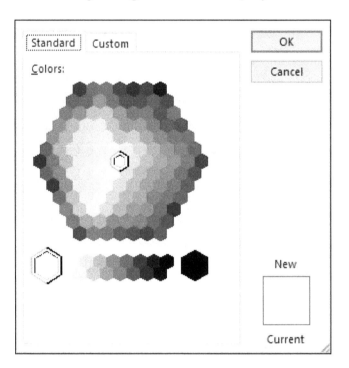 More Colors...

The following dialog box will be displayed:

The first tab (labeled **Standard**) allows you to select from a group of predefined colors.

The box in the lower right corner of the dialog box will display the current font color as well as the new color you select.

The second color tab (labeled **Custom**) allows you to further customize the color applied to the text, as shown below:

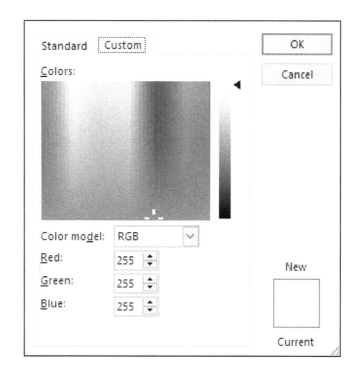

Unless you know the exact values for a particular color, follow the steps shown below to choose a custom color:

❶ Click or tap in the palette area on the color to customize. Notice the bottom right corner of the screen contains a box labeled **Current**. Be sure you see the color to customize in that box before continuing to the second step.

❷ Drag the color marker ◄ up or down to intensify the color. Notice the **New** color box at the bottom of the dialog box.

❸ Once you have the desired color, click or tap on the ‾OK‾ button to close the dialog box.

CHANGING CASE

If you created a text object after having pressed the  key by mistake, you can have PowerPoint go back and convert the text to the correct case.

Select the text object to be converted.

Aa ▾   Click or tap on the **Change Case** tool (located within the Font section on the Home Ribbon).

> Sentence case.
>
> lowercase
>
> UPPERCASE
>
> Capitalize Each Word
>
> tOGGLE cASE

The following choices are available within this list:

Sentence case	The first character of each sentence will be capitalized. PowerPoint looks for punctuation (a period, exclamation or question mark) to determine the end of a sentence.
lowercase	Converts selected text to all lowercase.
UPPERCASE	Coverts selected text to all uppercase.
Capitalize Each Word	Capitalizes the first letter of each word.
tOGGLE cASE	Switches the case of the selected text to the exact opposite as it is now.

Select the desired case from the list.

APPLYING MULTIPLE ATTRIBUTES

If you need to change several attributes, it might be faster to access the Font dialog box and do it all at once.

Click or tap on the **Font Dialog Box Launcher** (located within the Font section on the Home Ribbon).

The first tab (labeled **Font**) offers the following options:

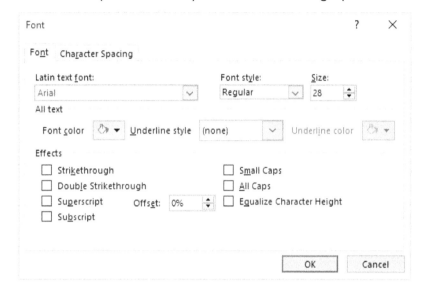

As you make changes within this dialog box, a preview of your selections is displayed at the bottom.

Latin text font	Scroll through the list of available fonts. They are listed in alphabetical order and contain the fonts currently installed on your system. Simply click/tap the font you would like to use.
Font style	Scroll through the list of font styles. The styles available will depend on the currently selected font. Click/tap on the style you want to apply.
Size	Scroll through the list of available font sizes. Click/tap on the size you want to apply.
Font color	Click or tap on this box to specify which font color to apply to your text.

Underline style   Click on this box to specify the type of underline you want to apply to your text.

Underline color   If you have chosen to underline text, you can click this box to specify which underline color you would like to apply to your text.

Effects   Use these checkboxes to specify which (if any) effects should be applied to your text. Click in its corresponding box (to enable it). To remove an unwanted effect, click a second time to remove the check (disabling it).

The tab labeled **Character Spacing** contains these options:

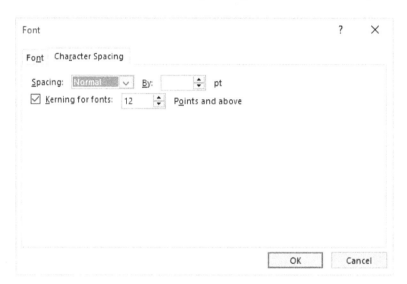

Spacing   Use this section to manually increase or decrease the spacing between the individual characters. Choose either Expanded or Condensed and then enter the amount in the box labeled **By**.

Kerning for fonts   Use this box to have PowerPoint automatically adjust the spacing between characters to give your words a more evenly spaced appearance.

When done, click or tap on [OK] to accept the changes made within the dialog box and return to your slide.

WORKING WITH THE MINI TOOLBAR

When you select a block of text, PowerPoint displays a semitransparent toolbar called the Mini toolbar. The Mini toolbar helps you work with fonts, font styles, font sizing, alignment, text color, indent levels, and bullet features.

When you see the transparent toolbar appear, simply point to the attribute you want to set and select it with your mouse.

REMOVING ATTRIBUTES

If you have applied several text attributes and then decide you want to remove them, PowerPoint includes a tool for that.

 After selecting the text containing the attributes you want removed, click or tap on the **Clear Formatting** tool (located within the **Font** section on the Home Ribbon).

ALIGNING TEXT

When working with text, PowerPoint is set for left alignment. To change the alignment, place your cursor anywhere within the paragraph you wish to adjust and then select one of the following tools (located within the **Paragraph** section of the Home Ribbon):

Left Aligned

Centered

Right Aligned

Full Justification

VERTICALLY ALIGNING TEXT

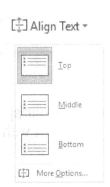

Click or tap on this tool (located within the **Paragraph** section of the Home Ribbon) to vertically align text on the slide. From the pull-down list, select the vertical alignment to be applied to the text on the current slide.

SETTING TEXT DIRECTION

Click or tap this tool (located within the **Paragraph** section of the Home Ribbon) to change the direction of the text on the slide. From the pull-down list, select the text direction you want to set for the selected text.

ADJUSTING LINE SPACING

You can also quickly adjust line spacing within a slide.

Click or tap this tool (located within the **Paragraph** section of the Home Ribbon). From the pull-down list, choose the line spacing to be applied to the selected text.

USING THE FORMAT PAINTER

USAGE:

PowerPoint offers a feature which allows you to copy attributes from one object and paste them onto another object.

To use the format painter, follow the steps outlined below:

❶ Select the text containing the attributes to be copied.

❷   *Format Painter*   Select the **Format Painter** tool from the Home Ribbon. If you plan on formatting more than one block of text, double-click or double-tap on this tool.

     Your mouse pointer changes to a paintbrush.

❸ Select the object to be formatted. PowerPoint will automatically apply the same formatting options you copied. If you only clicked the tool once, PowerPoint deactivates this feature after the first object is formatted.

❹ If you double-clicked or double-tapped the icon to begin with, continue highlighting each additional object to be formatted.

The Format Painter remains active until you deactivate it by clicking or tapping the tool again.

PRACTICE EXERCISE

Instructions:	❶	Move to slide number 13 in the presentation.
	❷	Select the president's box and change the font to Arial, bold, italic. Using the size tool on the tool bar, change the size of the text to 18.
	❸	Select the vice presidents and change the font to Arial, bold and change the font color to black. Using the size tool on the tool bar, change the size of the text to 16.

Module Three

- ● **Creating a New Presentation**
- ● **Creating a Title Chart**
- ● **Saving & Printing Charts**
- ● **Modifying Text Charts**
- ● **Working with Bullet Lists**

STARTING A NEW PRESENTATION

USAGE:

You will obviously be creating new presentations and not just working on existing ones. You can either create a presentation from scratch or use one of your own existing files to base the new presentation on. In addition, you can base the new presentation on one of PowerPoint's built-in templates. For example, if you want to create a marketing presentation, you could use PowerPoint's template and then edit it to include your specific information. Using a template can save you a great deal of preparation time.

To create a new presentation, select **New** from the pull-down list of options within the File tab on the Ribbon.

The following window will be displayed:

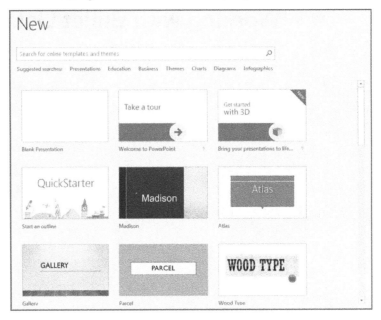

You can create a blank presentation or base the new file on one of the built-in templates that come with PowerPoint. A template is used to determine the basic structure of the presentation and can contain predefined settings, such as colors, fonts, layouts, graphics, formatting, and macros.

When you click on one of the templates, a pop-up window is displayed with a preview of the template. Within the preview, you might have additional template images that you can view and/or additional themes to choose from.

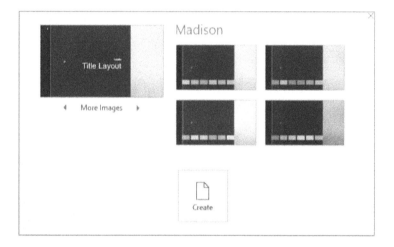

If there are templates that you'll be using on a regular basis, you may want to pin them to the list so that they remain at the top for easy access. To quickly pin a template, point to the template and then click or tap on 📌. If you change your mind, click or tap the 📌 icon to unpin the template.

 If you decide you'd like to use the selected template, click or tap on this button (within the preview screen).

The new presentation will be created - based on the template you have selected.

NOTE: *To quickly create a new blank presentation without first having to access the Office menu, press CTRL + N.*

OUTLINING YOUR PRESENTATION

USAGE:

Use the outline pane (located to the left of the slide) to start the "brainstorming" portion of your presentation.

Outline
View

Click or tap this icon (located within the **Presentation Views** section of the View Ribbon) to access the Outline View.

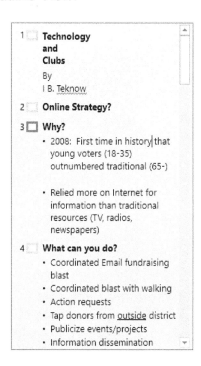

This pane is great for quickly creating new slides, rearranging slides or entering the bullet items for a slide. Entering text is also easiest through the use of the outline.

> *TIP:*   *To increase the size of the outline pane, place the mouse pointer on the vertical line separating the slide and outline pane. The pointer will change to a 2-way arrow ⟺. Hold down the [LEFT] mouse button and drag the mouse right to increase the outline pane.*

To the left of each title is the slide number and slide icon. The slide number indicates the order in which the slide will be displayed within the presentation.

DISPLAY/HIDE SLIDE DETAILS

To display/hide the details of a slide, simply double-click or double-tap on the slide icon (just to the left of the slide title in the outline pane). If you double-click or double-tap a second time on the slide icon, the slide will hide the details.

ADDING A NEW SLIDE

When adding a new slide within PowerPoint, the new slide is added after the current slide.

New
Slide ▾

To add a new slide while working in outline view, select the slide **after** which you want the new slide to appear and then use this button (located within the **Slides** section of the Home Ribbon).

To create a new blank slide, click on the top half of the button. Click or tap on the bottom half to specify the layout for the slide you are creating.

PROMOTING/DEMOTING TOPICS

When working with slides containing bullet or number lists, you can change the outline level of a particular item by promoting/demoting it. Promoting an item refers to raising its hierarchy level within the outline by outdenting the item. Demoting refers to lowering an item's hierarchy level within the outline by indenting the item.

The quickest method for promoting or demoting topics within a bullet or numbered list is to use the indent ⫶ or outdent ⫶ tool (located within the **Paragraph** section of the Home Ribbon).

You can also press [TAB] to demote a topic or press [SHIFT]+[TAB] to promote a topic.

REARRANGING SLIDES WITHIN THE PRESENTATION

Since you will typically access the outline pane to "brainstorm" a new presentation, you may find that some slides/topics should be rearranged in a different order.

To move a slide up/down in the outline, move the mouse pointer over the icon of the slide to be moved. When the mouse pointer changes to a four-way arrow click on the slide's icon and drag the entire slide up or down.

As you drag your mouse up or down, you will see a light horizontal line move with your mouse pointer. The line indicates where the slide will be placed when you let go of the mouse button.

When you reach the location where the slide should be inserted, release the mouse button.

REARRANGING TOPICS

You can also move the individual topics of a slide in a different order or even to different slide. You can use the same methods you use to move slides. The only difference is that you drag the bullet of the item to be moved.

REMOVING A SLIDE/BULLET

The quickest method for removing an unwanted slide or bullet while editing is to switch to Outline, select the item and press DEL.

ADDING HEADERS & FOOTERS

USAGE:

You can add footers to your slides that include the date, slide number and custom text. In addition, notes and handouts can also include a header.

A header appears at the top of pages whereas a footer is added to the bottom of a page.

It is best to add your headers and footers before beginning work on your slides so that you can adjust the placement of your objects so that they do not interfere with your headers and footers.

Header & Footer

Click or tap this button (located within the **Text** section of the Insert Ribbon) to add your headers and footers.

The following dialog box will be displayed:

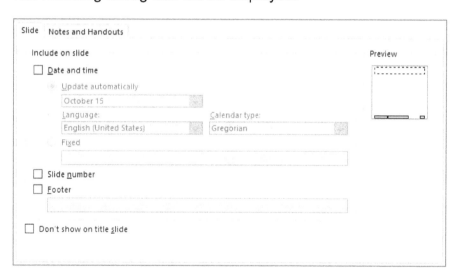

The tab labeled **Slide** is used to define the footer to be displayed at the bottom of each slide.

Check the box labeled **Date and time** to print the date and time along the left side of the footer. You can choose to have PowerPoint automatically update the date and time to the current setting each time you open the presentation or you can choose to enter a fixed date that will never change. You can also select a different display language as well as a different calendar type.

Check the box labeled **Slide number** to include the current slide number along the right side of the footer.

In the box labeled **Footer**, enter any custom text you would like to include.

The checkbox along the bottom left of the dialog box (labeled **Don't show on title slide**) is used to omit the footer from the title slide.

Click or tap Apply to apply the footer to the current slide. Click or tap on Apply to All to apply the footer to all slides within your presentation.

You can select the tab labeled **Notes and Handouts** if you want to create and customize a header or footer for your Speaker Note pages and Audience Handouts.

Using this second tab, you can include the date and time, and any custom text for the header as well as the page number and custom footer text.

WORKING WITH TEXT CHARTS

USAGE:

Text charts in PowerPoint are charts made up solely of text. They have no graphs included but may include logos and other clipart.

Text charts make up 70% of most presentations and are extremely useful in presenting topics in a brief, yet readable manner.

The following rules should be followed when creating text charts:

- ➢ Focus on one main point

- ➢ Use short words and phrases

- ➢ No more than 5 or 6 words/line

- ➢ No more than 5 or 6 lines/chart

- ➢ Mix upper and lowercase for readability

There are several different types of text charts. You can create as many of each as needed.

ENTERING TEXT

Entering text on a slide is simple. If you are working within the outline pane, simply type the text on the slide you are working with. You can make editing changes needed by using `←BACKSPACE` and `DEL`.

If you are working within the slide pane, it is a little different. Most PowerPoint charts have pre-defined sections, called "place holders" for titles and bullet lists. The place holders have dashed borders similar to the one shown below:

> ### Click to add title

Click or tap in the box. A flashing cursor will appear, indicating you may now begin to type. Place holders have default settings that affect the text font, color and other text characteristics. You can change the format for that text block at any time, but it will only affect that one block on that slide, not all slides. The default settings for all place holders can only be changed on the Slide Master.

USING THE TEXT BOX TOOL

If you want to place text on a slide where there is no placeholder (maybe for a caption or note), follow the steps outlined below:

❶ | A | Click or tap on this tool (located within the **Text** section on the Insert Ribbon). The mouse pointer changes to an upside down cross ↓

    Text Box

❷ Click or tap in the location where you want to place the text. A small flashing cursor will appear, indicating that you may begin typing. The text will not wrap so you will need to press `ENTER` to start a new line.

NOTE:	To have the text constrained within a certain area, drag a box on the slide after you have selected this tool. The width of the box determines the margins. Once you have the box, you can begin typing.

FINDING TEXT

If you need to locate a word or group of words you entered on a slide but cannot remember which slide you entered the word(s) on, you can use the "Find" feature to have PowerPoint locate the word for you.

$\mathcal{P}$ Find   Click or tap on this button (located within the **Editing** section of the Home Ribbon).

The following dialog box will be displayed:

In the box labeled **Find what** enter the text you want to locate.

Notice you can choose to have PowerPoint match the exact case and/or locate whole words only.

Click or tap Find Next to locate the first occurrence of the word(s). PowerPoint takes you to the first match and highlights it.

The dialog box remains on the screen so that you can continue searching through the presentation.

You may have to drag the dialog box away from the slide so you can see the highlighted word.

REPLACING TEXT

If you decide you would like to replace the word you have been searching for with another word, click on Replace... .

The dialog box will be expanded, as shown below:

In the box labeled **Replace with**, enter the replacement text.

Click or tap Replace... to replace the first instance of the word and move to the next, giving you complete control over which words will be replaced.

Click or tap Replace All to replace all words within one sweep without asking for confirmation.

When you are done, choose Close to close the dialog box.

CHANGING THE SLIDE LAYOUT

You can quickly switch slide layouts (i.e., change from a title chart to a bullet list) by following the steps outlined below:

❶ Select the slide to be modified.

❷ ▦ Layout ▾   Click or tap this button (located within the **Slides** section of the Home Ribbon).

❸
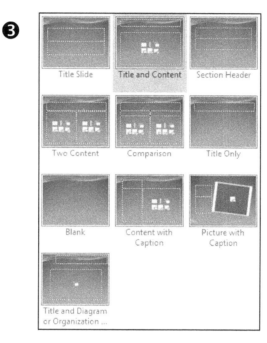
From the pull-down list of available layouts, select the one you would like applied to the currently selected slide.

RESETTING A SLIDE

If you have been playing around and changing the attributes of a slide and decide you would now like to have it return to its original format, you can instruct PowerPoint to reset the slide.

 Reset   Click or tap this button (located within the **Slides** section of the Home Ribbon) to reset the position, size, and formatting of the slide placeholders to their default setting.

SAVING A PRESENTATION

USAGE:

After having created a presentation, you will want to save it using a name that will allow you to easily find it again. If you access the File tab (across the top of the screen in the ribbon section), you will notice two options for saving a presentation: **Save** and **Save As**.

Save is the normal save feature which will ask you the first time you save a file to assign a name to it. From that point on, choosing SAVE will simply update the file to include the new information. On the other hand, **Save As** saves an existing file under a new name or as a different format to be imported into another program.

 Click or tap the **Save** icon (located on the Quick Access Bar).

When you first save a presentation, you will need to specify where you want to save it:

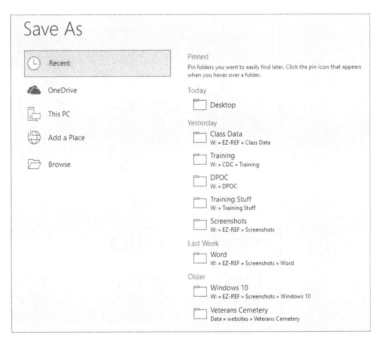

 Recent — Use this to save the presentation in a folder that has been recently used.

 OneDrive

 OneDrive - Personal
he@va.com

Use this to store the file in your Microsoft OneDrive account instead of your local computer. This allows you to access the file from anywhere. If you are already logged in, you'll see the bottom option.

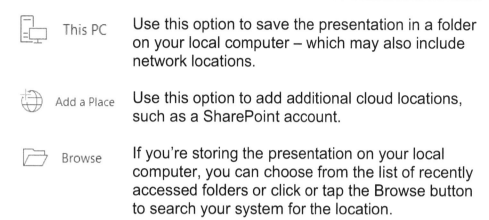

This PC   Use this option to save the presentation in a folder on your local computer – which may also include network locations.

Add a Place   Use this option to add additional cloud locations, such as a SharePoint account.

Browse   If you're storing the presentation on your local computer, you can choose from the list of recently accessed folders or click or tap the Browse button to search your system for the location.

Once you select a storage location, you will be taken to the dialog box that will prompt you to enter a file name, as shown below:

Along the left side of the dialog box, PowerPoint displays the **Navigation Pane**. This pane lists common/favorite locations (links) as well as a section for browsing your folders and drives.

Use the option in the bottom left corner to hide/display the "Folders List" section at the top of this window.

Use the address bar to determine the path, as shown below:

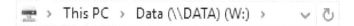

Notice the path is displayed horizontally on the bar. For example, in the diagram shown above the currently selected item is the "Data" drive (W) which is available on your computer. To get to that folder, you had to first go to "This PC", then the Data drive (W).

This layout is commonly referred to as "bread crumbs" because it shows you the path that was taken to get to the current location.

You can easily move to another folder on the "W" drive by clicking or tapping on the ⟩ arrow beside the drive name and then selecting a different folder to view.

In the box provided, enter a name for the new file. Letters, numbers and spaces are allowed. Enter 1-255 characters.

Notice that PowerPoint defaults to assigning the "pptx" extension.

If you want to save the presentation in another format (such as a previous version of PowerPoint so that someone else can edit the presentation who does not have this version), click on the down arrow ⌄ beside the box labeled **Save as type** and select the format from the list provided.

Enter a name for the presentation in the box labeled **File name** and then click or tap on ⌐ Save ¬ to actually save the file.

| TIP: | The shortcut key for saving is ⟦CTRL⟧+⟦S⟧. |

PRINTING

USAGE:

Obviously, an important part to any presentation is the ability to print the slides you have created.

Click or tap on the **File** tab on the Ribbon and select **Print** from the pull-down list of options.

The Print window will be displayed:

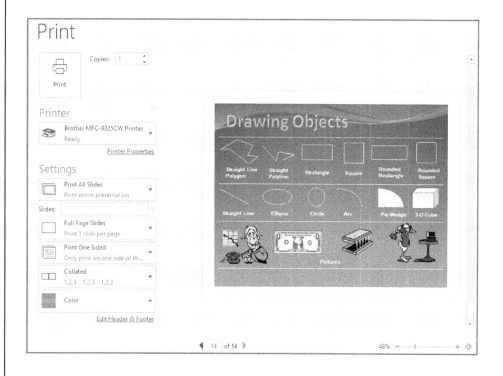

A preview of the presentation as it will be printed appears along the right side of this window.

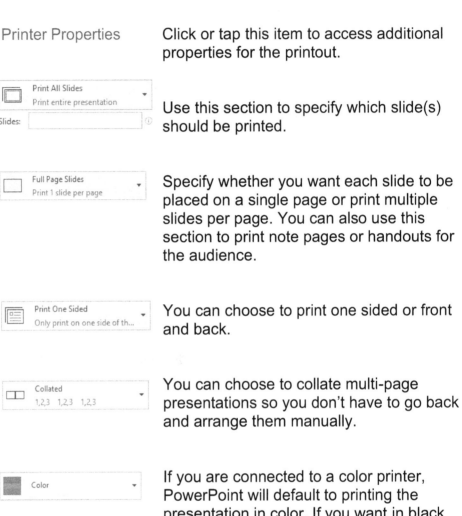

Click or tap on this button to select the printer you want to use.

Click or tap this item to access additional properties for the printout.

Use this section to specify which slide(s) should be printed.

Specify whether you want each slide to be placed on a single page or print multiple slides per page. You can also use this section to print note pages or handouts for the audience.

You can choose to print one sided or front and back.

You can choose to collate multi-page presentations so you don't have to go back and arrange them manually.

If you are connected to a color printer, PowerPoint will default to printing the presentation in color. If you want in black and white or grayscale, use this button to change the current setting.

Allows you to customize the header/footer.

Click or tap this button to begin printing.

TIP: The shortcut key for printing is *CTRL* + *P*.

ADDING/DELETING SLIDES

USAGE:

As you develop your presentation, you will obviously need to add new slides, but you may also want to delete a slide.

ADDING A NEW SLIDE

PowerPoint adds new slides **<u>after</u>** the current slide. Before you add a slide, be sure the slide you want the new slide to come after is displayed. For example, if you want a new slide number 5, the current slide number 4 should be displayed on the screen.

To add a new slide, follow the steps outlined below:

❶ Select the slide that should come before the new one you are about to add.

❷ New Slide ▾ Click or tap on this button (located within the **Slides** section of the Home Ribbon). If you click on the top portion of the button, you will be creating a new blank slide. If you want to specify the layout for the new slide, be sure to click on the bottom half of the button.

TIP:	*Notice once you are in the new slide that PowerPoint displays a series of objects in the middle of the slide which can be selected and therefore added to the new slide. Objects include tables, charts, Smart Art graphics, pictures, online pictures, and media clips.*

DELETING A SLIDE

There will obviously be times when a slide is no longer required/wanted in your presentation and, therefore, will need to be removed.

Follow these steps to remove an unwanted slide:

❶   Switch to Slide Sorter view.

❷   Select the slide(s) you wish to remove.

❸   Press the DEL key.

NOTE:	You will not be asked to confirm the deletion! However, if you change your mind after deleting a slide, click or tap the ↺ button (located on the Quick Access toolbar at the top of your screen).

WORKING WITH BULLET LISTS

USAGE:

Bullet lists are used to introduce or summarize specific points within a presentation. Bullets can be numbers or symbols. Bullet lists may be included on existing slides or can be added as a new slide to your presentation.

There are a few rules which should be adhered to when creating presentations containing bullet lists:

➤ Use no more than 5 or 6 bullets per list
➤ Begin with the same part of speech (e.g., noun or verb)
➤ Use either all phrases or sentences
➤ Follow capitalization and punctuation styles
➤ Use the same shape for all bullets to ensure uniformity
➤ Make bullet points approximately the same length

CONVERTING A BLOCK OF TEXT TO A BULLET LIST

To convert an existing block of text to a bullet list, follow these steps:

❶ Click or tap within the block of text to be converted to a bullet list.

❷ Click or tap a second time - this time on the border surrounding the block of text so that all text lines within the text box will be selected.

TIP:	*If you want to add a bullet to a single line, simply select the line to which the bullet should be added.*

❸ Click or tap one of these tools (located within the **Paragraph** section of the Home Ribbon).

HIDING/SHOWING BULLETS

You can choose to hide or display individual bullets within the list or you can remove all of the bullets from a bullet list.

You can use one of these tools (located within the **Paragraph** section of the Home Ribbon) to add or remove the bullet from the current text line.

If you want to hide/show the bullets from an entire block, select the block first, and then click on the bullet tool.

ADDING A BULLET LIST TO AN EXISTING CHART

To add a bullet list to an existing chart, follow the steps below:

❶   Select the **Textbox** tool (located within the **Text** section of the Insert Ribbon).

❷   Position the pointer where the bullet list should begin.

❸   If you want the bullet list to be constrained within margins, drag the mouse to size the text box to the desired width.

❹   When you release the mouse button, a cursor will appear inside the text box.

❺   Click or tap on one of these tools (located within the **Paragraph** section of the Home Ribbon).

❻   Begin typing the bullet points.

❼   Press ENTER for each new bullet point.

(OPTIONAL)

INDENTING A BULLET POINT

If you need to add sub-topics to your bullet list, you can easily indent (demote) a bullet point using the mouse or keyboard, as shown below:

Click or tap this button (located within the **Paragraph** section of the Home Ribbon) to demote the bullet one level.

You can also press [TAB] to indent (demote) a bullet point. However, you must have the cursor at the beginning of the line.

OUTDENTING A BULLET POINT

If you indented (demoted) a bullet point and would like to now outdent (promote) it, you can do so using either the mouse or keyboard, as shown below:

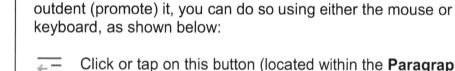

Click or tap on this button (located within the **Paragraph** section of the Home Ribbon) to promote the bullet one level.

Use [SHIFT]+[TAB] to outdent (promote) a bullet point. However, you must have the cursor at the beginning of the line.

MOVING A BULLET POINT UP/DOWN

Use [ALT]+[SHIFT]+[↑] to move a bullet point up the list.
Use [ALT]+[SHIFT]+[↓] to move a bullet point down the list.

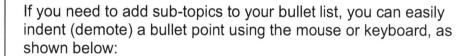

CHANGING THE BULLET STYLE

You can customize the bullet points by simply selecting the line whose bullet should be changed. Each line can have a different bullet style.

NOTE:	To customize the default bullets assigned to a particular bullet slide template, you will need to modify the Slide Master for that template. Once modified, each new slide based on that template will automatically include the new bullet style.

To change the bullet style, follow the steps outlined below:

❶   Select the bullet point line(s) to be modified.

❷   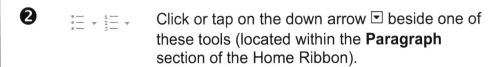 Click or tap on the down arrow ⊡ beside one of these tools (located within the **Paragraph** section of the Home Ribbon).

❸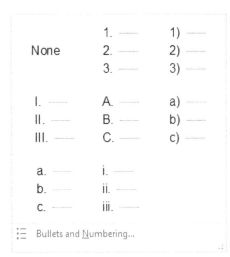

From the pull-down list, select the new bullet style you would like applied.

To further customize the bullet, choose the bottom option labeled **Bullets and Numbering...** which will take you to a dialog box where you can change the size and color of the bullet or even select a picture to be used as a bullet.

PRACTICE EXERCISE

Instructions:

❶ Create a new presentation based on a "business sales strategy" template.

❷ Using the new presentation, add the following slides to the end:

Afternoon Session

Sales Strategies
Current Income Sources
Sales Analysis

Sales Strategies

Methods for Increasing Sales

◆ Red Light Sales
◆ Two Day Sale - This Weekend Only
◆ Buy one - get one free!
◆ Free Cheapo Gifts with Purchase

Module Four

- **Drawing Objects & Shapes**
- **Inserting Online Pictures**
- **WordArt & SmartArt**
- **Adding Charts & Tables**
- **Formatting Charts & Tables**

DRAWING OBJECTS

USAGE:

As you begin creating slides, you will find that many items will have to be drawn manually. PowerPoint provides several tools which give you the capabilities to create complex drawings, as discussed on the next several pages.

 **DRAWING LINES**

❶ Point to the **Line** tool (located within the **Drawing** section of the Home Ribbon) and click or tap. The mouse pointer changes to a cross-hair.

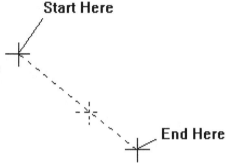

❷ Move to where you want the line to begin and drag to where the line should end.

❸ Notice as you drag the line's ending point, you can adjust the direction and length as needed by moving the mouse around.

TIP: *To draw a line to the nearest 45-degree angle, hold the* SHIFT *key down while dragging!*

TIP: *By default, PowerPoint allows you to draw only one object at a time. If you want to draw several lines, you must select the tool again.*

○ DRAWING AN OVAL/CIRCLE

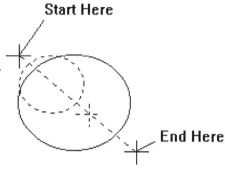

❶ Point to the **Oval** tool (located within the **Drawing** section of the Home Ribbon) and click or tap.

❷ Position the cross-hair pointer at one corner of an imaginary box surrounding the oval.

❸ Drag the pointer to the far corner of the oval.

❹ Notice as you drag, the shape and size of the oval adjusts accordingly.

TIP:	To create the oval whose center remains at the starting point, hold down the CTRL key as you drag the mouse. Be sure to release the mouse before letting go of the CTRL key! To create a circle, hold down the SHIFT key while dragging. Be sure to release the mouse before letting go of the SHIFT key!

TIP:	If you simply click the [LEFT] mouse button once (within the drawing area) after selecting the oval tool, PowerPoint will create a one-inch circle!

☐ **DRAWING RECTANGLES/SQUARES**

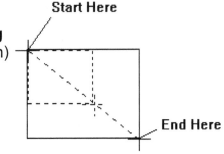

Start Here

End Here

❶ Point to the **Rectangle** tool (located within the **Drawing** section of the Home Ribbon) and click or tap.

❷ Position the pointer where the top left corner of the rectangle should begin.

❸ Drag to the position where the bottom right corner of the rectangle should appear.

❹ Notice as you drag, the shape and size of the rectangle adjusts accordingly.

TIP:	*To draw a rectangle from its center point, hold the **CTRL** key down while dragging the mouse. Be sure to release the mouse before letting go of the **CTRL** key!*
	*To draw a square, hold the **SHIFT** key down while dragging. Be sure to release the mouse before letting go of the **SHIFT** key!*
	*To draw a square from its center, use both the **CTRL** and **SHIFT** keys while dragging.*

TIP:	*If you simply click the [LEFT] mouse button once (within the drawing area) after selecting the rectangle tool, PowerPoint will create a one-inch square!*

DRAWING SHAPES

In addition to creating lines, ovals, and rectangles PowerPoint also allows you to add predefined shapes to your slides.

These shapes consist of such items as triangles, arrows, scribbles, arcs, curves, braces, and stars.

To add one of these shapes to your slide, follow these steps:

❶ Select the shape you want to create (from the list located within the **Drawing** section of the Home Ribbon.

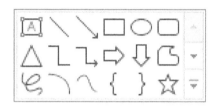

❷ If you're using a mouse, notice the mouse pointer has changed to a cross-hair. Position the cross-hair pointer where the top left corner of the shape should begin.

❸ Drag to the position and size where the bottom right corner of the shape should appear.

❹ Notice as you drag, the shape and size of the object adjusts accordingly.

ACCESSING THE COMPLETE LIST OF SHAPES

If none of the shapes within the Shapes section meet your needs, click or tap on the ▽ button in the bottom right corner of the Shapes section to display the complete list of available shapes.

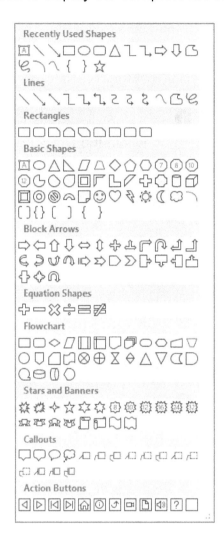

INSERTING ICONS

In addition to shapes, PowerPoint allows you to insert icons to visually communicate via easily recognized images.

To insert an icon, click on this tool (from within the **Illustrations** section of the Insert Ribbon).

The following window will be displayed:

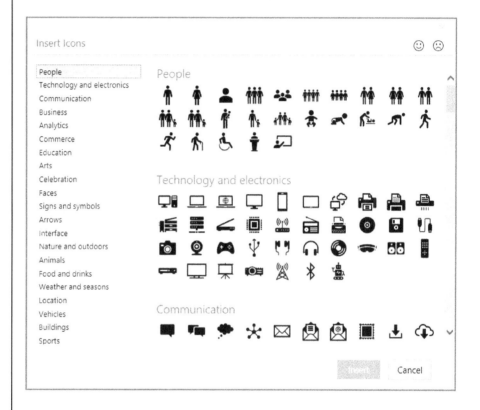

From the left side of the window, select the category of icon you want to use and then select the actual icon from the right side.

Select the icon(s) you want to add to your presentation. A checkmark will be placed bedside each selected icon.

Click on the Insert button to add them to the current slide.

Once inserted, you can change the color, size, etc. just as you would any other shape within your presentation.

Text
Box

USING THE TEXT TOOL

Follow the steps outlined below to add a block of text to a slide:

❶   Point to the **Text Box** tool (located within the **Drawing** section of the Home Ribbon) and click or tap. If you're using a mouse, notice the mouse pointer has changed to an upside-down cross ⊥.

❷   If you position the pointer where the text should appear and click or tap, a text box will be created without margins. Text will continue to be added on a single line. You will need to press the `ENTER` key to start a new line.

If you want the text box to be a specific size, drag the mouse to size the text box to the desired width. Text will automatically wrap to the next line when your cursor reaches the right border of the text box. This will allow you to continuously type text without having to press the `ENTER` key to start a new line of text.

❸   When you see the flashing cursor, begin typing in the text.

❹   When you are done entering the desired text, click away from the text box.

NOTE:	*Once you have inserted text, you can modify it by changing the font, font size, and apply text attributes (such as bold and italics) by accessing the formatting tool bar towards the top of the screen.*

USING THE RULER

USAGE:

When working with a slide, you will often want to position items in a specific location. In order to be precise, you need to turn on the ruler so that you know where you will be placing the item.

 Ruler Check this box (located within the **Show/Hide** section of the View Ribbon) to display the ruler.

SETTING TABS

When working with text objects, you might find it useful to create tabs for aligning your text. Tabs are used for creating columnar lists of numbers and text. The default tabs are set for every inch.

PowerPoint allows you to create four types of tabs: Left, Center, Right, and Decimal. An example of each is listed below:

Left Tab	Center Tab	Right Tab	Decimal Tab
100	100	100	100
1000	1000	1000	1000
10	10	10	10
1.00	1.00	1.00	1.00
100.000	100.000	100.000	100.000
10.0	10.0	10.0	10.0

When editing text, the left edge of the ruler contains an icon ⬛ used to select the type of tab or indent required.

⬛	Left Tab	Text is left-aligned under the tab.
⬛	Center Tab	Text is centered under the tab.
⬛	Right Tab	Text is right-aligned under the tab.
⬛	Decimal Tab	This is used for numerical data. The decimal point in the value (number) lines up under the tab.
⬛	First Line Indent	Adjusts the indent of the first line of a paragraph.
⬛	Hanging Indent	Adjusts the rest of the paragraph (the body), allowing you to create hanging indents.

To set a tab, follow these two steps:

❶   Choose the appropriate tab style and then move to the position on the ruler where the tab should be inserted.

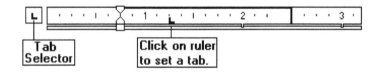

❷   Click the **[LEFT]** mouse button once and the tab will appear.

REMOVING TABS FROM THE RULER

Grab the tab stop and pull it off the ruler.

MOVING A TAB STOP POSITION

Grab the tab stop and drag it to the new location.

DRAWING OPTIONS

USAGE:

There are many advanced drawing options within PowerPoint, as discussed on the next several pages.

ROTATING OBJECTS

PowerPoint makes it easy for you to position objects in the exact angle you need.

❶   Select the object you want to rotate.

❷   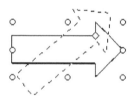 Point to the rotation handle (which is automatically displayed above the selected object). The pointer will change to a rotation icon (↻).

❸   Click and drag to rotate the selected object. As you drag, the mouse pointer will change shape again ( ).

Drag the handle in the direction you want to rotate.

❹   When you are finished, let go and the object will be redrawn in its new position.

ADJUSTING SHAPES

Many of the AutoShapes have an extra adjustment handle in the shape of an orange circle .

You can use this to adjust some aspect of the shape such as the thickness of an arrowhead, three-dimensional depth and other features.

This adjustment handle is not used to change the size of the shape but rather the most prominent feature of the shape.

The exact adjustment feature will depend on the selected shape.

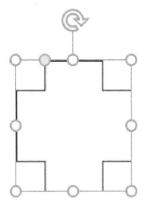

To adjust the shape, follow the steps outlined below:

❶   Place the mouse pointer over the orange adjustment handle. The mouse pointer will change to a smaller arrow (▷).

❷   Drag the handle in the direction you want. You will see an outline of the new shape to help you decide when to stop.

❸   Once the adjustment is made, release the mouse button.

ATTACHING TEXT TO A SHAPE

To add text to a shape, simply select the shape and begin typing. By default, PowerPoint will keep the original size of the shape but will allow the text to spill outside of the shape.

If the text spills out over the shape you can either select the text and change its size or change the size of the shape to accommodate the text.

You can also change the font, font size, color, and any other text attributes just as you would any other text object on a slide. Select the text and then choose the font/size/attribute from the **Font** section of the Home Ribbon.

When you select a block of text, PowerPoint displays a semitransparent toolbar called the Mini toolbar. The Mini toolbar helps you work with fonts, font styles, font sizing, alignment, text color, indent levels, and bullet features.

When you see the transparent toolbar appear, simply point to the attribute you want to set and select it with your mouse.

ALIGNING TEXT WITHIN A SHAPE

When you add text to a shape, PowerPoint automatically aligns it along the left side. To change the alignment, place your cursor anywhere within the text and select one of the following tools (located on the **Home Ribbon**):

Left

Center

Right

Justify

ADDING A TABLE

USAGE:

At some point, you may need to include a list of columns and rows of tabular data on one of your slides. Instead of trying to create tabs to line the data up, you can insert a **Table** on the current slide.

The structure of a table consists of rows, which run horizontally, and columns, which run vertically. The intersections between these rows and columns are referred to as **cells**.

To add a table, move to the slide you want to place the table on and then click or tap this button (located within the **Tables** section of the Insert Ribbon).

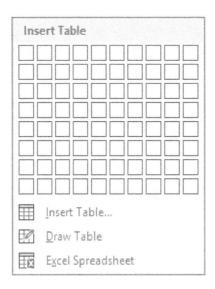

Highlight the number of columns and rows for the table.

If you were to choose "Insert Table…" from the pull-down menu you'd be taken to a small box where you could simply type the number or columns and rows for the table.

Notice you can choose to draw the table yourself.

You can also embed an Excel spreadsheet. If you choose to embed a spreadsheet, you will make changes to the spreadsheet directly from within Excel but simply display it here on the slide. To edit the object, you will double-click on it which will run Excel.

CREATING A NEW TABLE SLIDE

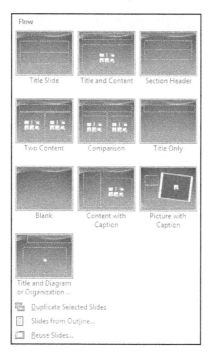 To create a new slide containing a table, click or tap this tool (located within the **Slides** section of the Home Ribbon).

From the list of available templates, choose one that contains a content section (displayed with a group of small colored icons).

Within the center portion of your new slide should be a group of icons representing objects that can be added to the slide:

Select ⊞ from the list of available objects.

You will be asked to enter the number of columns and rows for the table, shown below:

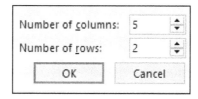

Select the number of columns and rows and click or tap ⬚ OK ⬚.

ENTERING TABLE DATA

Click in the cell you want to enter text in and begin typing.

To move to the next cell, press [TAB] or click with the mouse. If you press [TAB] while in the last cell of the table, PowerPoint will automatically add a new row.

Press [SHIFT]+[TAB] to move back one cell at a time.

APPLYING CELL ATTRIBUTES

You can also apply any of the text attributes to text within the table as you would any other text object within PowerPoint.

Simply switch back to the **Home Ribbon** select the text to be modified and then access the tools within the Font section.

CHANGING THE TABLE STYLE

Once the table has been created, PowerPoint automatically switches to the **Design Ribbon** for you to enhance the look of the table. Notice in the middle of this tab is a section labeled Table Styles. Use this section to change the style applied to your table.

Use the buttons to scroll up and down through the list of available styles. Click or tap on to display all of the styles within a single box.

ADDING CELL SHADING

To change the shading within a cell or group of cells, follow the steps outlined below:

❶   Select the cell(s) to modify.

❷   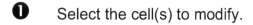   Click or tap on the down arrow ⊡ beside the **Shading** tool.

❸   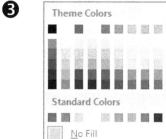   From the pull-down list, select the shading color to apply.

If you don't see the color you are looking for in the list, select **More Fill Colors...** to display the entire palette.

The pull-down may also list recently used colors.

Notice you can also add a picture, a gradient, or texture as the cell background.

ADDING BORDERS

To add borders to a cell or group of cells, follow these steps:

❶   Select the cell(s) to modify.

❷   Click or tap on the down arrow ⊡ beside the **Borders** tool.

❸      From the pull-down list, select the type of border to be applied.

CHANGING THE PEN STYLE

By default, when you choose to add a border, PowerPoint applies the last color, style, and weight (thickness) used.

If you want to add a border with a different color, style, or weight, you will need to first change the pen settings before applying the border. To change the pen style, follow these steps:

❶    Click or tap on the down arrow ⊡ beside the **Line Style** tool.

❷    From the pull-down list, select the pen style to apply to the next border you add.

PowerPoint changes your cursor to a pencil ✏ which you can now use to 'draw' the borders you want.

If you would rather not draw the borders, use the ⊞ Borders ▾ tool.

CHANGING THE PEN WEIGHT

To change the weight (thickness) of the pen for the next border you apply, follow these steps:

❶ 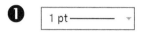 Click or tap on the down arrow ⊡ beside the **Pen Weight** tool.

❷ 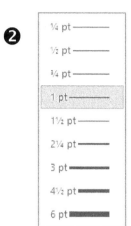 From the pull-down list, select a new pen weight to apply to the next border you add.

PowerPoint changes your cursor to a pencil ✎ which you can now use to 'draw' the borders with the new pen weight. If you would rather not draw the borders, use the ⊞ Borders ▾ tool.

CHANGING THE PEN COLOR

To change the pen color for the next border, follow these steps:

❶  Click or tap the **Pen Color** tool.

❷ 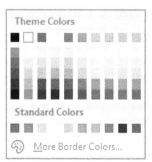 Select the color to apply from the pull-down list.

The pull-down may also list recently used colors.

If you don't see the color you want to apply, choose **More Border Colors...**

PowerPoint changes your cursor to a pencil ✎ which you can now use to 'draw' the borders with the new pen color. If you would rather not draw the borders, use the ⊞ Borders ▾ tool.

ADDING SPECIAL EFFECTS

To add special effects to a cell or group of cells, follow these steps:

❶ Select the cell(s) to modify.

❷ 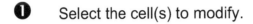 Click or tap on the down arrow ⊡ beside the **Effects** tool.

❸ From the pull-down list, select the type of effect to be applied.

MERGING CELLS

If you wish to combine two or more cells into a single one, you can use the eraser tool to "erase" the boundaries between the cells you want to combine (merge).

❶ 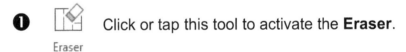 Click or tap this tool to activate the **Eraser**.

❷ Move within the table structure. Notice that the mouse pointer has changed to an eraser ✎. Click or tap on the boundaries between the cells to be merged.

❸ 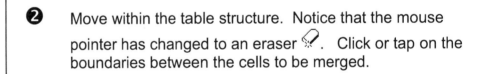 When you are done using the eraser, click or tap on this tool a second time to turn it off.

SPLITTING CELLS

You can split a single cell into multiple cells by following the steps outlined below:

❶ Click or tap this tool once to select the **Draw Table** option.

Draw Table

❷ Move within the table structure. Notice that the mouse pointer has changed to a pencil ✎. Use the pencil to draw the borders within the cell you wish to split. PowerPoint applies the last used pen style, weight, and color to the new borders you are drawing.

❸ When done, click or tap on this tool a second time to stop drawing.

Draw Table

MOVING A TABLE

Like any other object on a slide, a table can be moved or resized.

To move the table, point to one of the borders surrounding it until you see the mouse pointer change to four-way arrow ✛ and then click and drag it to a new location.

RESIZING THE TABLE

To resize the table, select the table and then point to one of the handles until you see a double-sided arrow ↔↕↘↙. Drag the handle to increase/decrease the size of the table.

DELETING A TABLE

To remove a table from your slide, simply select it and press [DEL].

WORKING WITH ONLINE PICTURES

USAGE:

If you do not feel comfortable creating your own drawings from scratch, you may decide to use PowerPoint's online picture library. PowerPoint uses Microsoft's Bing search engine to search for images online.

INSERTING ONLINE PICTURES

To insert an online picture, follow the steps outlined below:

❶

Online
Pictures

Click or tap on the **Online Pictures** tool (located within the **Illustrations** section of the Insert Ribbon).

A window displays categories of available clip art to choose from, as shown below:

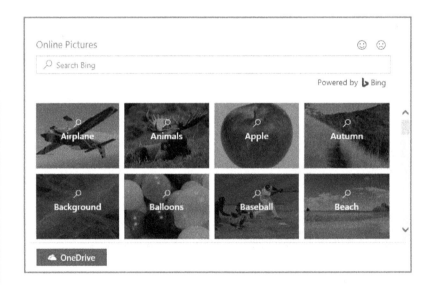

❷ In the box provided, select a category or type in the keyword(s) that best defines what type of picture you are looking for.

PowerPoint will search through its libraries and online to locate pictures that best match the search criteria you have entered and display them for you, as shown below:

By default, Bing displays pictures it 'assumes' are free to use. However, you are still responsible for ensuring you have permission to use the selected picture.

❸   Double-click or double-tap on the picture you wish to insert

or select it and click or tap on the   Insert   button.

Once the picture has been placed on the slide, you can manipulate it (e.g., change its size and placement) just as you would any other drawing object.

REMOVING AN ONLINE PICTURE

To remove a picture from your presentation, follow the two steps outlined below:

❶   Click or tap on the picture to select it.

❷   Press DEL

WORKING WITH WORDART

USAGE:

PowerPoint offers a feature which allows you to create text objects that use fancy special effects. This can greatly enhance your slide and make title slides, in particular, appear much more professional.

❶

Click or tap on this button (located within the **Text** section of the Insert Ribbon) to add a WordArt object to your slide.

A pull-down list of WordArt styles will appear:

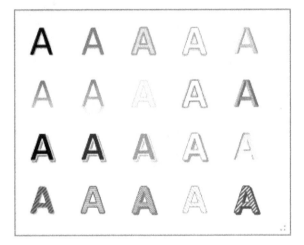

❷ From the list, select the WordArt style you wish to apply. The colors and styles in the list will vary depending on the theme of the current presentation.

A new object will be placed on the slide:

❸ Enter the text within the box provided.

CHANGING OUTLINE COLOR AND STYLE

To modify the color applied to the outline surrounding the WordArt object as well as the style of the outline, follow the steps below:

❶ Select the WordArt object.

❷ ✏ Shape Outline ▾   Click or tap this button (located within the **Shape Styles** section of the Format Ribbon).

❸
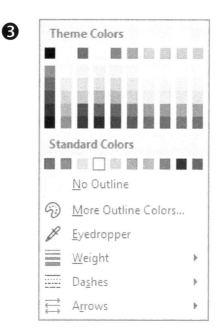

From this pull-down list, you can choose a new outline color, remove the outline altogether, change the weight of the outline, and change the style of the line to include dashes or arrows.

The pull-down may also list recently used colors.

If you do not see the desired color from the list, select **More Outline Colors...** which displays the entire color palette.

Notice as you move your mouse over each of the options within the list, PowerPoint provides a preview of the selected WordArt object using the option you are currently pointing to.

CHANGING FILL COLORS

To modify the fill color, picture, gradient, and texture applied to the box surrounding a WordArt object, follow the steps outlined below:

❶   Select the WordArt object to be modified.

❷    Click or tap on this button (located within the **Shape Styles** section on the Format Ribbon).

❸   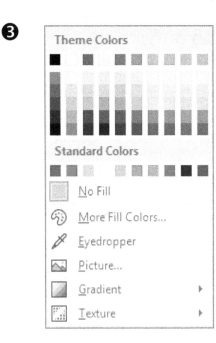   From this pull-down list, you can choose a new fill color, remove the fill altogether, or change the fill to include a picture, a gradient, or a texture.

In addition to **Theme** and **Standard Colors**, this pull-down may list recently used colors.

If you do not see the desired color from the list, select **More Fill Colors...** which displays the entire color palette.

Notice as you move your mouse over each of the options within the list, PowerPoint provides a preview of the selected WordArt object using the option you are currently pointing to.

A gradient typically consists of two colors gradually blending from one color to the other. You can select the colors to be used as well as the intensity and the direction in which the gradient will be generated.

Textures are basically small patches of patterns that resemble real-life textures such as marble, cloth, grass, paper, wood, etc.

Rather than using one of the built-in textures or patterns, you can choose to fill a WordArt object with a custom picture. PowerPoint recognizes most graphic file formats to provide you with a wide variety of options.

Microsoft PowerPoint for Office 365

ADDING A SHAPE EFFECT

Adding a shape effect (such as a shadow or a bevel effect) can give the WordArt object a more custom look and feel to help it to stand out from the rest of the drawing.

To apply a shape effect to a WordArt object, follow these steps:

❶ Select the WordArt object to be modified.

❷  Click or tap on this button (located within the **Shape Styles** section on the Format Ribbon).

❸  From this pull-down list, choose the shape effect you wish to apply to the selected object.

Notice as you move your mouse over each of the options within the list, PowerPoint provides a preview of the selected WordArt object using the option you are currently pointing to.

The options in the pull-down list are:
Preset, Shadow, Reflection, Glow, Soft Edges, Bevel, 3-D Rotation

USING A PREDEFINED SHAPE FOR WORD ART

Rather than using the individual shape tools to customize the Word Art object, you can use one of the predefined shapes by following the steps below:

❶   Select the WordArt object to be modified.

❷   Use the section shown below (located within the **Shape Styles** section of the Format Ribbon).

Use the  buttons to scroll up and down through the list of available styles. Click or tap on ⊽ to display all of the shapes within a single box.

CHANGING THE WORD ART STYLE

You can also choose a different style for the text by following the steps outlined below:

❶   Select the WordArt object to be modified.

❷   Use the section shown below (located within the **WordArt Styles** section of the Format Ribbon).

Use the ⬍ buttons to scroll up and down through the list of available styles. Click or tap on ⊽ to display all of the text styles within a single box.

CHANGING TEXT FILL

To change the text fill of the WordArt object, follow these steps:

❶ Select the WordArt object to be modified.

❷ Click or tap this tool (located within the **WordArt Styles** section of the Format Ribbon).

❸ 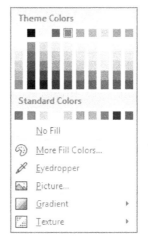 In addition to **Theme** and **Standard Colors**, this pull-down may also list recently used colors.

From this pull-down list, choose the text fill color to be applied.

CHANGING TEXT OULINE

To change the text outline of a WordArt object, follow these steps:

❶ Select the WordArt object to be modified.

❷  Click or tap on this tool (located within the **WordArt Styles** section of the Format Ribbon).

❸ 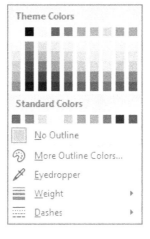 In addition to **Theme** and **Standard Colors**, this pull-down may also list recently used colors.

From this pull-down list, choose the text outline color to be applied.

CHANGING TEXT EFFECTS

To change the text effects applied to the WordArt object, follow these steps:

❶ Select the WordArt object to be modified.

❷  Click or tap on this tool (located within the **WordArt Styles** section of the Format Ribbon).

❸ 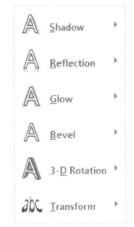 From this pull-down list, choose the text effect to be applied.

PRACTICE EXERCISE

Instructions:	❶	Create a drawing similar to the one shown below.
	❷	Notice that clipart has been added to the drawing.

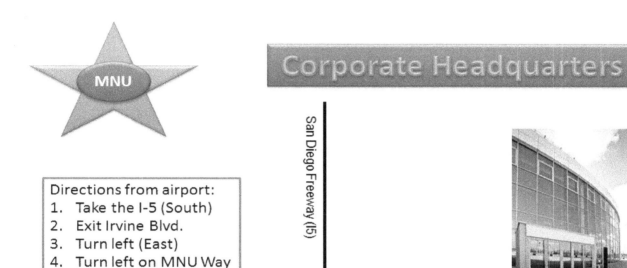

WORKING WITH SMARTART

USAGE:

SmartArt is a special type of graphic that can take lists of text and create unique charts (such as organizational, matrix, cycle, and pyramid charts) from the data.

❶ 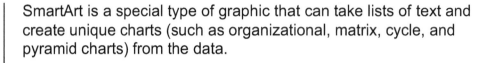 SmartArt

Click or tap this tool (located within the **Illustrations** section of the Insert Ribbon) to add a SmartArt chart to your slide.

A box containing various SmartArt styles will appear:

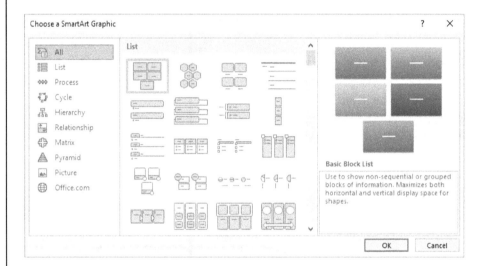

The left side of the dialog box contains a list of available chart categories. The middle section of the box changes to display the available styles within the selected chart category.

If you select one of the styles within the middle section of the box, the right side displays a sample and brief description of that chart.

❷ From the list, select the SmartArt chart style you want to create and then click or tap OK .

A new chart will be placed on the slide:

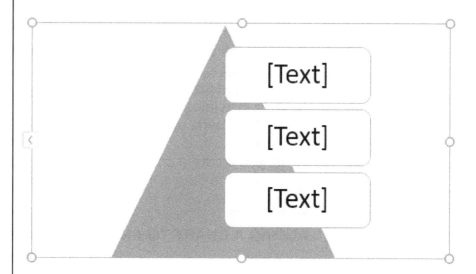

❸ Click or tap in one of the text sections within the chart to enter your text.

Notice there is also an outline box along the left side of the chart where you can also enter the information for your chart:

 ⟨ If you don't see this box, click or tap this button (located along the left side of the chart).

To change the look or style of the chart, access the Design Ribbon.

WORKING WITH CHARTS

USAGE:

Presentations usually include a set of numbers representing some point that the speaker is trying to get across to the audience (e.g., sales figures, statistical information). Most audience members, however, find that looking at a series of numbers is boring and seem to lose interest in the presentation when a slide contains only numbers. Charts allow you to visually represent numbers.

When you create a chart within PowerPoint, Excel automatically is run so that the data is input through a spreadsheet and then plotted/charted within PowerPoint.

ADDING A CHART TO AN EXISTING SLIDE

❶ Click or tap on this tool (located within the **Illustrations** section of the Insert Ribbon).

The following window will be displayed:

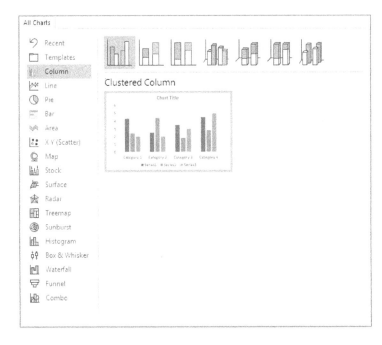

PowerPoint lists the various chart categories down the left side while the right side of the window displays the types of charts available within the selected category. When you move your mouse over a sample chart, PowerPoint will offer a more detailed view of that chart type.

❷ Select the type of chart to create and click/tap ☐ OK .

EDITING THE CHART

Once the chart has been added to your slide, you can edit it using the Ribbon across the top of your screen and the three new tools that appear whenever the chart is selected:

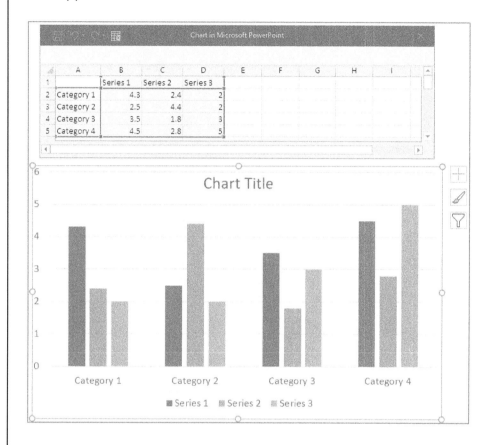

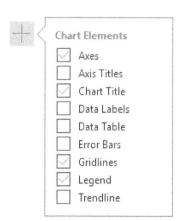

The **Chart Elements** tool allows you to add, remove or change the titles, axes, legend, gridlines and data labels.

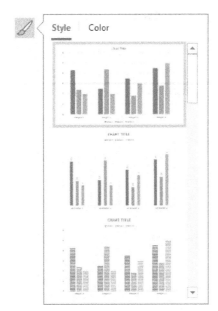

The **Chart Styles** tool is used to apply styles and define a color scheme for the selected chart.

The **Chart Filters** tool defines what values within the worksheet are being plotted within the chart.

ADDING A CHART TITLE

Across the top of the chart you should see a generic title. Click on that title to customize it. You can then select the title and access the **Font** section of the Home Ribbon to change the font, font size, font color, and text attributes for the chart title.

CHANGING THE TYPE OF CHART

Once you have created your chart, you may decide you should have selected a different type. For example, you should use bar/line graphs if you need to show relationships, comparisons or correlations.

Line graphs in particular should be used to display a trend. For example, you would use a line graph if you want to plot the trend in sales over the past few quarters/years. The lines would allow the viewer to easily see the current trend in sales.

Change
Chart Type

Click or tap this tool (located within the **Type** section of the Design Ribbon) to change the type of chart.

You will be returned to the original box where you can choose a different type of chart to apply.

EDITING DATA

Edit
Data ▾

If you somehow close the worksheet window or can't find it, select the chart and then click or tap this tool (located within the **Data** section of the Chart Tools Design Ribbon). If you click on the down arrow, you'll have the option of editing the data within the PowerPoint worksheet or opening it within Excel.

PARTS OF A CHART

Each bar/line chart can consist of either a single series or multiple series. PowerPoint allows you to plot several series.

PowerPoint refers to these graphs as **XY** because they are made up of an x-axis (the horizontal axis consisting of the category indicators) and a y-axis (the vertical axis containing the values being plotted). The y-axis can be located on the left (y1) or right side (y2) of the chart. Some charts contain both a y1 and y2 axis.

A sample bar chart is displayed in the diagram below:

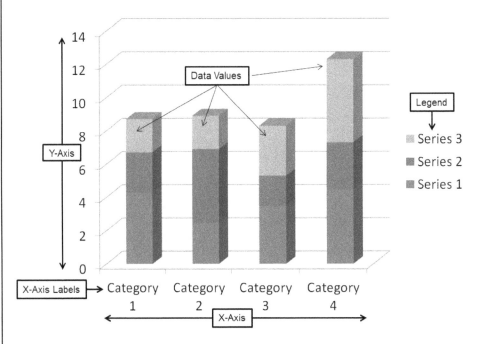

Each data value is represented by a bar on the graph and is identified by a "label" along the x-axis.

On the other hand, you would use pie charts if you need to show parts of a whole. Pie charts show each data item as an individual part of the total value. For example, use a pie chart if you have a list of expenses and would like to see how much each individual expense contributes to the total amount.

Each pie chart consists of a single set of data values. For example, you can have a pie chart that displays expenses, but a pie chart with expenses <u>and</u> income categories combined would not make much sense as neither category contributes to the other.

Each pie has a set of labels that identifies each slice and a set of values for each slice, as illustrated in the diagram below:

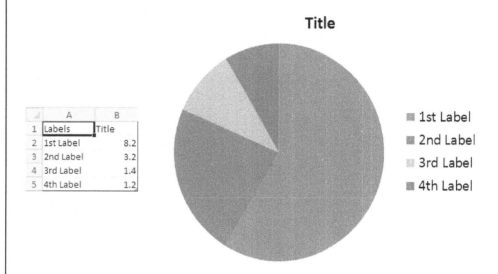

The spreadsheet to the left is used to enter the different data labels and values for the chart.

Each value should have a name or "label" assigned to it so that it can be identified on the chart. Notice how each slice represents a small part of the total value.

To modify the data, click or tap on the data form to activate it.

Once activated, you would use the first row and first column to enter the data series and category names.

SELECTING CHART OBJECTS

To select various chart objects, click on the item (x-axis labels, y-axis labels, legend, data series, chart title, etc.). Handles will surround the selected item.

To modify a text object, simply select the object and then access the **Font** section of the Home Ribbon.

To change the fill color, line color, style or effects for a data series, simply select the series and then access the **Drawing** section of the Home Ribbon.

CHANGING THE CHART STYLE

Use the section shown below (within the **Chart Styles** section of the Chart Tools Design Ribbon) to choose a different chart style.

CHANGING THE CHART LAYOUT

Click or tap on this tool (located within the **Chart Layouts** section of the Design Ribbon) to choose a different chart layout.

SIZING THE CHART

To size the chart, follow the steps outlined below:

❶ Click on any of the outside borders surrounding the chart. Be sure you see the handles around the chart.

❷ ⟷⇕⤡⤢ Place the tip of your mouse pointer on one of the handles. The pointer changes to a double-sided arrow. Click and drag the **[LEFT]** mouse button to resize the chart.

❸ When done, release the mouse button.

MOVING THE LEGEND

It is also possible to move the legend to a more appropriate location, if desired. To do so, select it and then drag it to a new location, as outlined in the steps below:

❶ Select the legend by clicking on it once. Be sure you see the handles surrounding the object.

❷ ✛ Move the mouse pointer to one of the borders surrounding the legend box until you see the four-way arrow. Click and hold the **[LEFT]** button down while dragging the legend to its new location.

❸ When you reach the desired location, release the mouse button.

APPLYING TEXT ATTRIBUTES TO CHART OBJECTS

You can quickly apply attributes to text within chart objects the same way you applied attributes to any text object.

Select the portion of the chart to be modified and then click or tap on one of the following tools (which are located within the Font section on the Home Ribbon):

B   Click or tap on this tool to turn **bold** on and off.

I   Click or tap this tool to turn *italics* on and off.

U ▾   Click or tap this tool to turn <u>underline</u> on and off.

CHANGING THE FONT OF CHART OBJECTS

You can change the font of a chart object just as you would any other cell.

Before continuing, select the chart object to modify.

❶   Click or tap on the down arrow ▾ beside the **Font** tool (located within the Font section on the Home Ribbon).

❷   Select the new font from the pull-down list.

CHANGING FONT SIZE

To quickly change the font size of an object on your chart, select the object and then click on the down arrow beside the **Font Size** tool (located within the Font section on the Home Ribbon). From the list provided, select the new size.

If you are unsure of the exact size you would like to select, you can use the following tools to incrementally change the font size:

A˄ A˅   Click or tap on these tools to quickly increase or decrease the current font size.

CHANGING THE FONT COLOR

You can quickly change the color of the font by selecting the text object and then accessing the ribbon, as shown below:

❶   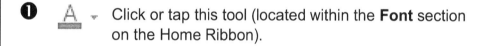 Click or tap this tool (located within the **Font** section on the Home Ribbon).

❷   Select the color you want to use (from the pull-down list) for the selected text.

APPLYING NUMERIC FORMATS TO CHART OBJECTS

The numbers along the axis are automatically formatted based on the cells within the worksheet. For example, if there are dollar signs ($) within the worksheet, PowerPoint will include them on the chart. However, if you need to reformat the numbers on the axis, follow these steps:

❶

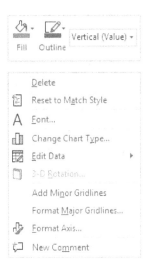

Right-click on the axis you want to format and choose **Format Axis**... from the pop-up menu.

❷

PowerPoint will open the Format Axis panel (along the right side of your screen). At the bottom of this panel, click on **Number** to reveal the numeric format options.

You can choose a format **Category** (such as currency, percentage, date) as well as the number of decimal places (if applicable) and/or currency **Symbol** (if applicable).

PowerPoint will update your chart as you make the selections within the Format Axis panel.

When you're done, click on the **X** (in the upper right corner) to close the panel.

CUSTOMIZING FILL EFFECTS

You can also customize the fill effects of a single series or the entire background of the chart, as outlined in the steps below:

❶ Select the series or background to be customized.

❷

Click or tap on the down arrow ⊡ to the right of this tool (located within the **Drawing** section of the Home Ribbon).

❸ In addition to **Theme** and **Standard Colors**, you may also see Recent Colors.

Select the fill color and or fill effect (picture, gradient, or texture) that you would like applied to the currently selected data series.

CUSTOMIZING THE OUTLINE

In addition to changing the fill effect, you can also change the outline of the bars on the chart by following these steps:

❶ Select the series or background to be customized.

❷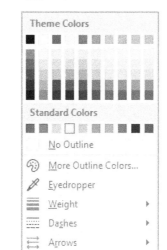

Click or tap the down arrow ⊡ to the right of this tool (located within the **Drawing** section of the Home Ribbon).

❸ Select the outline color, weight, and style for the currently selected data series.

ADDING A SHAPE EFFECT

Adding a shape effect (such as a shadow or a bevel effect) can give a series of bars or columns on the chart a more custom look and feel to help it to stand out.

To apply a shape effect to a data series, follow the steps below:

❶ Select the data series to be modified.

❷ ⬭ Shape Effects ▾   Click or tap this button (located within the **Drawing** section on the Home Ribbon).

❸

☐ Preset ▸
☐ Shadow ▸
☐ Reflection ▸
☐ Glow ▸
☐ Soft Edges ▸
☐ Bevel ▸
⬚ 3-D Rotation ▸

From this pull-down list, choose the shape effect you wish to apply to the selected data series.

Notice as you move your mouse over each of the options within the list, PowerPoint provides a preview of the selected data series using the option you are currently pointing to.

PRACTICE EXERCISE

Instructions:	❶	Create a sales chart as close to the one shown below.

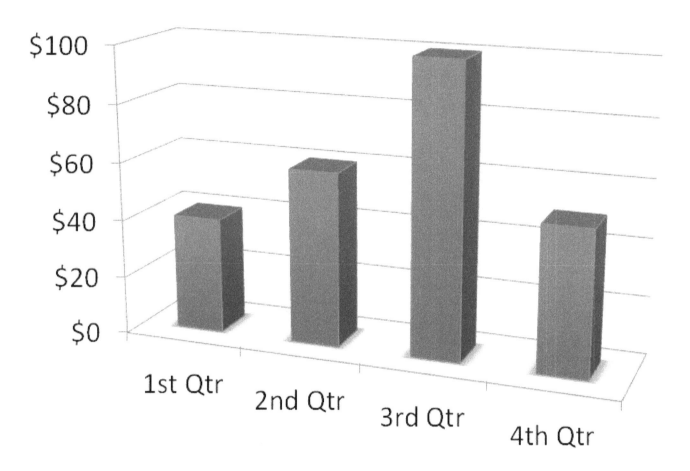

PRACTICE EXERCISE

Instructions: Create a pie chart as close to the one shown below.

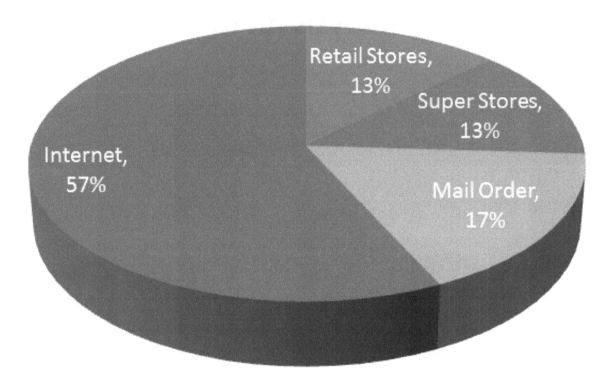

Module Five

- **Creating a Slide Show**
- **Adding Special Effects**

CREATING A SLIDE SHOW

USAGE:

A slide show is a desktop presentation. They are most often used when presenting information to an audience. Slide shows can be instrumental in conveying a message to a group of people. You can connect your PC to an overhead and display the show to a large group. It can run in the background as you speak to the audience or you can add enough special effects that the show itself is sufficient in conveying the point you are trying to make.

Rather than simply showing the audience a variety of slides, adding animation and special effects give the presentation added appeal to hold the audience's attention while still making a dramatic point.

It is possible to control the show using either the keyboard or the mouse. It can be a self-running demonstration or can run interactively with the audience depending on your requirements.

□□ Click or tap on this button (located with the other view
□□ buttons along the bottom right side of the screen) to access the **Slide Sorter** view. You can then rearrange your slides by dragging them back and forth to new positions.

ADDING TRANSITION EFFECTS

To add a transition effect, follow the steps shown below:

❶ Select the slide(s) you want to add a transition effect to.

❷ Click or tap on one of the transition effects listed below (located within the **Transition to this Slide** section on the Transitions Ribbon).

Use the ⬍ buttons to scroll up and down through the list.
Click or tap ▾ to display all of the transitions in a single box.

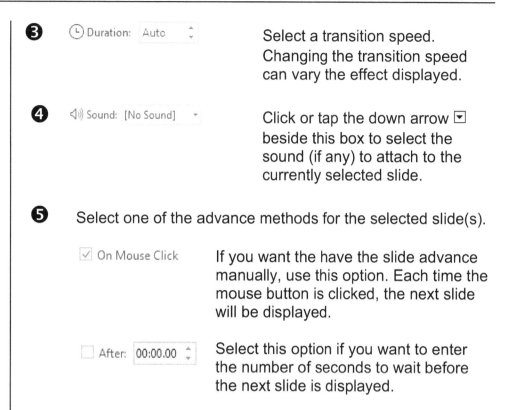

❸   Select a transition speed. Changing the transition speed can vary the effect displayed.

❹   Click or tap the down arrow ⊡ beside this box to select the sound (if any) to attach to the currently selected slide.

❺   Select one of the advance methods for the selected slide(s).

     ☑ On Mouse Click   If you want the have the slide advance manually, use this option. Each time the mouse button is clicked, the next slide will be displayed.

     ☐ After: 00:00.00   Select this option if you want to enter the number of seconds to wait before the next slide is displayed.

To review the settings you have just selected, click or tap on Preview to view the current slide with its transition effects. This is the same as clicking or tapping on the ⁃★ button (located just beneath the left side of the slide while working within the sorter view).

TIP:	To apply the same settings (e.g., transition effect, transition speed, transition sound) to all of your slides, click or tap on the 🔲 Apply To All button.

REHEARSE TIMINGS FOR THE SLIDE SHOW

You also can rehearse your speech for each slide and have the time recorded so that a slide stays on the screen for the duration.

 Rehearse Timings

Click or tap this tool (located within the **Setup** section on the Slide Show Ribbon) to rehearse slide timings.

The slide show will begin and a small toolbar will be placed in the top left corner of the screen, as shown below:

Notice there are two counters on the toolbar. The counter in the middle of the toolbar is used to specify the amount of time for the current slide to remain on the screen during the slide show whereas the counter along the right side of the toolbar displays the total running time for the entire slide show.

Notice there's a checkbox labeled "Use Rehearsed Timings". Remove the check if you decide not to use the timings you set.

HIDING A SLIDE

If you decide one of your slides should not be included within the slide show, you can have PowerPoint hide it.

Hide Slide

Click or tap on this button to hide the current slide when running the slide show.

PLAYING THE SLIDE SHOW

Once the effects have been assigned, you can run the slide show.

From Beginning

Click or tap this tool to run the slide show from the beginning.

From Current Slide

Click or tap on this tool to run the show from the currently selected slide.

ADDING ANIMATION TO TEXT AND OBJECTS

To further customize a block of text or other object on your slide, you can add animation to it. This can be useful to draw attention to a specific point on your slide.

To assign an animation effect to a block of text or an object, follow the steps outlined below:

❶   Switch back to the Normal view. Select the item on the slide you wish to animate.

❷   Choose one of the animation effects (from the **Animation** section on the Animations Ribbon). If you don't see one in the list provided, click or tap on ⊟ to expand the list.

CHANGING THE ANIMATION EFFECTS

Depending on the animation you select, there may be different effects to choose from. For example, having the text fly in from the left side of the screen rather than the right side, etc.

Effect
Options ▾

Once you have selected the animation you want to use, click or tap on this tool to choose the effect. The icon for this tool will change, depending on the animation that you've selected.

The options within the pull-down list will vary depending on the animation you have selected.

PRACTICE EXERCISE

Instructions:	❶	Create a slide show using the slides created during class.
	❷	Customize the show by adding a different effect to each slide.
	❸	Be sure to save the presentation when you are done.

Module Six

- **Accessing the Master**
- **Creating a Background**
- **Themes**
- **Working with Templates**
- **Sharing Your Presentation**

ACCESSING THE MASTER

USAGE:

When creating a presentation within PowerPoint, you may find that you would like to add a company logo or graphic object that will be seen on each and every slide.

You can also specify the font and attributes to be applied to text objects. In addition, you can define the color, shape and size of bullets. By adding an object to each slide or deciding on a font/bullet style, you are able to give the presentation uniformity.

You must be careful, however, when adding background objects to existing presentations because these objects can interfere with text and/or other objects already on a slide. For this reason, it is better to create the background **before** you begin adding slides.

PowerPoint has three masters which can be accessed: Slides Master, Handout Master, and Notes Master.

Choose the **Slide Master** to specify the font, attributes and bullet styles applied to each type of slide. You may also add background graphics to this master.

Select **Handout Master** to determine the number and size of slides placed on audience handouts.

Select **Notes Master** to set the size of the area to be used when speaker notes are added to the slide. You can also specify the font, point size and any attributes to be applied to the notes text.

To edit one of these masters, switch to the View Ribbon.

Click or tap this tool (on the View Ribbon) to switch to the **Slide Master**.

Slide
Master

A new ribbon is added to the screen labeled "Slide Master." You can apply a new theme to the master as well as modify the colors, fonts, and effects of the current theme. You can also customize the background and change the page setup.

This ribbon also allows you to insert new placeholders for other chart objects you'd like to include on all slides. Notice the checkboxes to hide/show the title and footer placeholders.

PowerPoint displays a Master for the entire presentation and a Master for each slide layout along the left side of the window. Changes made to the Master presentation slide (font, background image, etc.) will affect all other slide layouts. Changes made to the individual Master slide layouts will only affect slides created using that layout. Select the slide layout you want to customize.

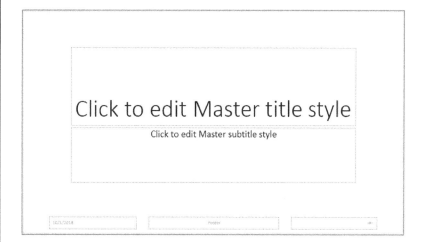

Once you select a slide layout, you will see placeholders for the different parts of that slide. For example, there will be a placeholder for the title, subtitle, chart objects, etc.

You can click or tap within any placeholder to define the default fonts and attributes to be applied to text contained in that section.

The bottom of the screen contains three small areas labeled **Date**, **Footer** and **#** (this references a page number). You may format the text and/or add your own text to these areas.

When done, click or tap on one of the view icons located towards the bottom right side of the screen or click/tap this button (located at the top of the window).

Close
Master View

CREATING A CUSTOM BACKGROUND

USAGE:

You can enhance your slides by applying a background color or pattern or even a picture to give them a more polished look. PowerPoint allows you to quickly add color or a graphic background to your presentation.

Background Styles ▾   While in the **Slide Master** view, click or tap on this tool (located on the Slide Master Ribbon).

A list of available backgrounds will be displayed, as shown below:

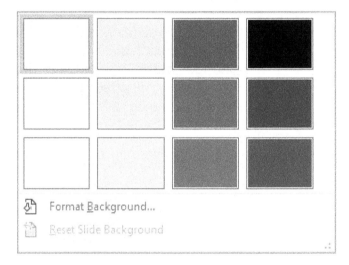

From the pull-down list, select one of the preset backgrounds or choose **Format Background…** to display a panel along the right side of the window where you can select a more custom background (such as a gradient, a texture, or a picture).

If you have already changed the background for a slide, notice the option within the pull-down list labeled **Reset Slide Background**.

If you have added pictures to the background but don't want them displayed on a specific slide layout master, you can hide them. This does not affect background colors or patterns.

☐ Hide Background Graphics   Click or tap on this tool (located on the Slide Master Ribbon) to hide the background graphic objects for the current slide layout.

WORKING WITH THEMES

USAGE:

You can format an entire presentation to give it a professional look by applying a theme from within the Slide Master view. A theme is a set of formatting choices that include theme colors, fonts (including heading and body text fonts), and theme effects (including lines and fill effects). Although you can quickly apply a theme directly from the Design Ribbon, you can customize the theme more effectively from within the Slide Master view.

 To apply one of the themes to the current presentation, click on this tool from the Slide Master Ribbon.

Themes

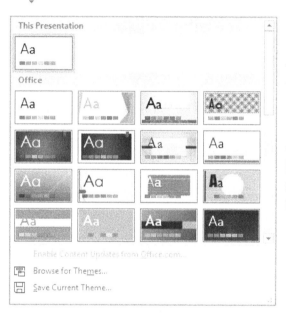

From the list of available themes, select the theme to be applied to your entire presentation.

Click or tap on the ⊟ button to expand the list and display all available themes.

To customize individual theme components, use these tools:

Colors ▾ — Customizes the theme colors being applied to your presentation. A list of theme colors will be displayed. Click on the one you want to apply. Notice you can also choose to create your own color theme.

Fonts ▾ — Customizes theme fonts applied to your presentation. A pull-down list of theme fonts will be displayed. Click or tap the one you want to apply to your presentation. Notice you can also create new theme fonts.

Effects ▾ — Customizes the theme effects being applied to your presentation. A pull-down list of theme effects will be displayed. Click or tap on the one you want to apply.

WORKING WITH TEMPLATES

USAGE:

PowerPoint allows you to customize your presentation by applying a template. Templates contain predefined color schemes, font styles, custom formatting, and slide masters that are designed to create a particular look and feel. You can use one of PowerPoint's many design templates or create your own.

The simplest method for defining a new template is to create a presentation as you would any other and then save it as a template.

Template files contain the extension **.POTX**. To create your own template, simply create a new presentation, enter the data and formatting codes that you would like stored with the template and then save the file as a template rather than the usual presentation. Once the template has been saved, you may create new presentations based on your template.

Each time you create a presentation based on a template, PowerPoint creates a brand new presentation (untitled until you save it) but places all of the text, objects, animations and formatting codes in that file based on the template.

PowerPoint needs to know what folder your personal templates will be stored in before you can create a new workbook based on your templates.

DEFINING YOUR TEMPLATE FOLDER

Although there shouldn't be a reason to change the default location for templates, to store your templates in a custom drive/folder, follow these steps:

❶   Select **Options** from within the File tab on the Ribbon.

❷ Select the **SAVE** option (along the left).

The following dialog box will be displayed:

💾 Customize how documents are saved.

Save presentations

☑ AutoSave OneDrive and SharePoint Online files by default on PowerPoint ⓘ

Save files in this format: ⌈ PowerPoint Presentation ▼ ⌉

☑ Save AutoRecover information every ⌈ 10 ⌉ minutes

    ☑ Keep the last AutoRecovered version if I close without saving

AutoRecover file location: ⌈ C:\Users\ezref\AppData\Roaming\Microsoft\PowerPoint\ ⌉

☐ Don't show the Backstage when opening or saving files with keyboard shortcuts

☑ Show additional places for saving, even if sign-in may be required.

☐ Save to Computer by default

Default local file location: ⌈ C:\Users\ezref\Documents\ ⌉

Default personal templates location: ⌈ ⌉

Offline editing options for document management server files

Saving checked out files to server drafts is no longer supported. Checked out files are now saved to the Office Document Cache.

Learn more

Server drafts location: ⌈ C:\Users\ezref\Documents\SharePoint Drafts\ ⌉

Preserve fidelity when sharing this presentation: ⌈ 📄 Presentation1 ▼ ⌉

☐ Embed fonts in the file ⓘ

    ⦿ Embed only the characters used in the presentation (best for reducing file size)

    ○ Embed all characters (best for editing by other people)

❸ Click or tap in the box labeled **Default personal templates location** and enter the exact location (drive and folder) where you will be storing your templates.

NOTE: *Since there's unfortunately no* ⌊ Browse... ⌋ *button in this box to search your system for the folder, you'll need to know the exact path yourself. A solution could be to click or tap on the* ⌊ Browse... ⌋ *button on the box labeled "Server drafts location" to locate the path and then copy and paste it in this box.*

❹ When done, click or tap ⌈ OK ⌉.

CREATING A NEW TEMPLATE

The simplest method for defining a new template is to create a presentation as you would any other and then save it as a template.

After creating the presentation and inserting all of the necessary information for the template, follow the steps outlined below to save it as a template for future presentations to be based on:

❶  Select **Save As** from the pull-down list of options within the File tab on the Ribbon.

The following window will be displayed:

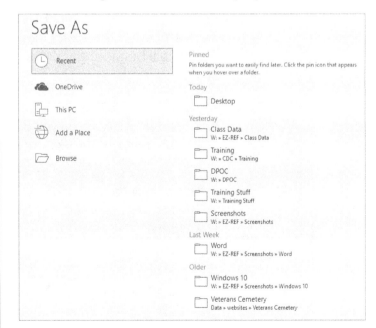

❷ Select a folder or click on 🗁 Browse

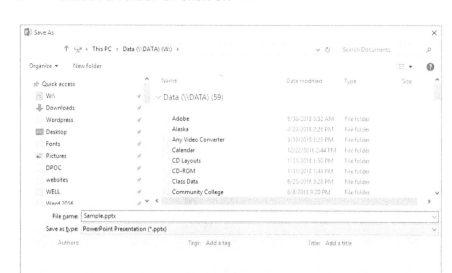

❸ In the resulting dialog box (shown below), click or tap on the down arrow ˅ beside the **Save as type** option and select "PowerPoint Template (*.potx)".

❹ Be sure you have entered a descriptive name for the template before clicking or tapping on [Save].

NOTE:	Notice that PowerPoint assigns the extension *.POTX* to template files.
	Normal Microsoft PowerPoint presentations are assigned the extension *.PPTX*.

USING A TEMPLATE

To use the template that you created, you will follow the usual steps to create a new presentation with one exception. You will choose your template as the one to base the new file on.

To create a new presentation based on an existing template, follow the steps outlined below.

    Select **New** from the File tab on the Ribbon.

The following window will be displayed:

❷ Notice that PowerPoint automatically displays the **Featured** templates (those created by Microsoft). Select **Personal** (from the top of the window) as the type of templates to be displayed.

❸ PowerPoint will change to display your personal templates. Select the one you wish to use by double-clicking on it.

A new presentation will be created – using the formatting defined in the selected template.

OPENING A TEMPLATE

If you realize that a template needs to be modified, you can open it as you would any other presentation. Once opened, you will be able to edit the template and then save it again. You can also edit the **Blank Presentation** template to set any defaults you would like applied to all presentations created using the default template.

To open a template, follow these steps:

❶  Select **Open** from the File tab on the Ribbon.

Your first step is to select where the template is stored:

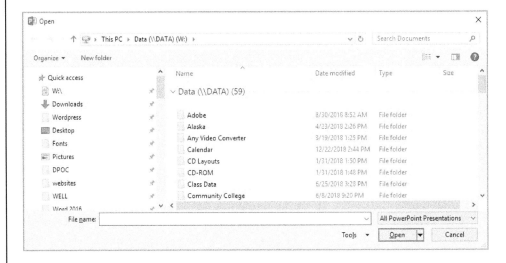 Browse   Click or tap this button to search your system for the folder storing the template.

The following dialog box will be displayed:

❸   Change the type of files being displayed (located towards the bottom right of the dialog box) to include only **PowerPoint templates (*.potx)**. You may need to switch drives/folders to locate it.

❹   Select the template to modify and choose Open.

Make the changes you'd like to the template and then save it again – as you would any other presentation.

SHARING A PRESENTATION

USAGE:

At some point, you will probably want to work on a presentation with another user or group of users. Simply sign in to your Microsoft Office account and then click on the Share icon to begin collaborating with others.

To share the current presentation, follow these steps:

❶ | Sign in | Click or tap on this tab (located on the ribbon across the top right portion of your screen) to sign in to your Microsoft Office account.

❷ You'll need to enter the email address or phone number of the account you want to use and then the password associated with your account.

❸ 🖃 Share Once you have signed in, click or tap this icon (located on the ribbon across the top right of your screen) to choose which user(s) will have access to the file.

PowerPoint will ask you to upload the document you want to share to OneDrive or you can attach the document (as a presentation or pdf file) to an email message.

Next, you'll be asked to invite people you want to collaborate with:

❹ As you add each user, you'll need to assign roles for each person you are collaborating with:

Use this panel to share the presentation with others and to assign permissions (whether the person you are sharing the file with can edit the presentation or just view it).

If you have an address book installed on your system, you can search for contacts by clicking on this button.

❺ After selecting the user(s) you wish to share this presentation with, click on the Share button.

PowerPoint will add the user's name to the list, as shown below:

An email will be sent to the user(s) you have invited with the name of the file being shared and a button to view it via OneDrive:

If you decide you need to remove or change the permissions for a shared user, right-click on their name and select an option from the pop-up menu that is displayed:

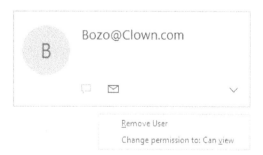

Appendix

- **Appendix A: Shortcut Keys**

APPENDIX A: SHORTCUT KEYS

KEYS:	ACTION:
CTRL + A	Select All
CTRL + B	Bold
CTRL + C	Copy
CTRL + D	Duplicate Slide
CTRL + E	Center
CTRL + F	Find
CTRL + H	Find & Replace
CTRL + I	Italics
CTRL + J	Justify
CTRL + K	Insert a Hyperlink
CTRL + M	Insert a New Slide
CTRL + L	Left Align
CTRL + N	New Presentation
CTRL + O	Open a File
CTRL + P	Print
CTRL + R	Right Align
CTRL + S	Save
CTRL + T	Customize Font
CTRL + U	Underline
CTRL + V	Paste
CTRL + W	Close File
CTRL + X	Cut
CTRL + Z	Undo
CTRL + SPACEBAR	Clear Character Formatting